```
roYal
chOsen
pecUliar
     sAnctified
     pRiesthood
     gEneration
          Nation
          hOly
          Transformed
               uNusual
               peOple
               diffeRent
               redeeMed
               ekklesiA
               caLled
```

SHAUN CAMPBELL

Copyright © 2016 by SHAUN CAMPBELL

YOU ARE NOT NORMAL
Dare To Be Different
by SHAUN CAMPBELL

Printed in the United States of America.

Edited by Xulon Press.

ISBN 9781498469593

All rights reserved solely by the author. The author guarantees all contents are original and do not infringe upon the legal rights of any other person or work. No part of this book may be reproduced in any form without the permission of the author. The views expressed in this book are not necessarily those of the publisher.

Unless otherwise indicated, Scripture quotations taken from the King James Version (KJV)–*public domain.*

www.xulonpress.com

To Missionary Shanelle

Thank you for your support

I pray this book is a blessing to you

God Bless

Dedication

I have written this book to encourage every young Christian, whether in age or in the faith and say to you that you are not alone. I have been where many of you are and by the grace of God and with the prayers of the saints, I am still standing. Although you are in the world, you are not of the world and you do not have to be like everyone else. You do not have to bow to the various pressures that you face. It is not an embarrassment to be a man or woman of God.

As a child of God, you are called to be different. I pray that this book will encourage, inspire, and challenge you to be all you can be for the Lord Jesus Christ. I pray that you fulfill the purpose for which you were born.

The Lord said that His Word would not return unto Him void (Is. 55:11), so the Word that He has spoken over your life *must* come to pass. He told Jeremiah that before he was formed in his mother's womb He knew him and ordained him to be a prophet (Jer. 1:5). The God of Jeremiah is still ordaining people before birth!

Acknowledgements

- First and foremost, I must give thanks to the Lord Jesus Christ for His inspiration and revelation. Thank you, Lord, for being the Friend that sticks closer than a brother. My desire is to be your friend; just as Abraham was called the friend of God (James 2:23), I too want to be your friend.
- To my wife Sheryl, you truly are a gift from God and my happily ever after. I appreciate you and love you from the bottom of my heart. Thank you for your encouragement, your support, and your love.
- To Dr. Annette Gilzene (Gilzene Dissertation and Thesis Editing), thank you for helping me with your outstanding editorial skills, for your patience, advice, and instruction.
- To Sylvia Burleigh, Nick Lopez, Michelle Johnston and the team at Xulon Press. Thank you for helping me accomplish a lifelong dream of publishing my first book.
- To Pastor Dawn Davis-Lawrence, thank you for your advice, encouragement, and support.
- To Minister Jeremy Grant, thank you for encouraging me to write this book. Although you didn't know it at the time, you once asked me when I was going to write the book entitled "Bro. Shaun's Spirit Filled Encouragement for Students?" Well Brother Jeremy, here it is!
- To my spiritual mothers and fathers in the Gospel. I cannot list you all here; however, here are the names

of just a few of my mothers and fathers who have set a positive example and have helped me over the years and continue to help me to this day. Thank you for being there for me when I needed you and thank you for your prayers and words of encouragement.

- o Overseer Eric Bailey
- o Mother Sylvia Evans
- o Elder Selvin Stone
- o Dr. Mavis Taylor
- o Bishop Leslie J. Barnes

- Last but not least, I would like to thank everyone who has encouraged me and prayed for me from my birth up until this day. I am a living witness that prayer works! This is the first of many books that I believe are within me and I hope and pray that all of them will be an encouragement to the body of Christ whether young, old, single, married; whether sitting on a rostrum or in the congregation.

Endorsements

If you or anyone you know has anything to do with youth ministry in this modern age, you will be greatly assisted by the contents of this book. *You Are Not Normal* could not have been written any sooner. These are, indeed, the days when folks, and especially our young people, are dealing with self-image issues, gender identity crises, peer pressure, and a plethora of complexities, which keep professionals in all fields on their ears.

In this timely masterpiece, Shaun Campbell has demonstrated that transparency and a deliberate injection of the undiluted Word of God, is the single most effective combination that can be employed in order to reach our youth and keep them committed to the Lord Jesus Christ, and to His church. The Bible stories chosen, and the explanations, which he provides, have also inspired my thinking even while reading the manuscript.

I have no doubt that *You Are Not Normal* is a book for this time and I unhesitatingly recommend it.

Pastor Carlton Christie
Pastor – Chosen Generation Ministries

I have known Shaun Campbell and his wife, Sheryl, for years and appreciate his passion and compassion for the Kingdom and the people of God. In a day where most of the church is surrendering to a narcissistic attitude to the work of ministry, he begins with the greatest call that can be made on a person's life–being a disciple! Not just a Christian.

If at your core, you desire to follow Jesus with all your heart, *You Are Not Normal* is a first step in that journey.

Elder Alan Todd
Pastor – Global Apostolic Ministries, Conference Speaker, Author of *The Church Made Flesh*

The idea of lifting the faith of your spiritual journey will make interesting reading and will seek to encourage and uplift lives as well. I personally endorsed the sentiments expressed and would recommend the book as an important part of anyone's reading collection.

Bishop Dr. C. A. Holdsworth
Senior Pastor – Greater Grace Temple, Kingston, Jamaica

If you're under the age of 25 you need to read this book, if you know someone under the age of 25 you need to buy him/her this book. *You Are Not Normal* brilliantly sets out, in easy to read chapters, what it means to be young and on fire for God. If you are wondering who you are in Christ and what it means to be a child of the King of kings, look no further. Discover why *You Are Not Normal*.

Elder Nick Myers
Bethel United Church of Jesus Christ Apostolic (Camberwell), London, UK

Unless otherwise stated, all Scripture quotations are taken from the King James Version of the Bible.

Contents

Introduction v

Chapter 1:   You Are Not Normal 19
Chapter 2:   The Call to Be Different 32
Chapter 3:   It Is Ok to Stand Out. 50
Chapter 4:   We Have a New Name 59
Chapter 5:   Presentation Is Important 64
Chapter 6:   What Do You See? 72
Chapter 7:   We Will Not Bow. .80

Conclusion. 92
Bibliography 94
About the Author. 95
End Notes. 97

Introduction

My name is Shaun Campbell. I am the youngest of four children born to my parents, Lawford and Dorcas Campbell. I prefer the term "youngest," firstly, because I am now thirty-eight years old, and secondly, being called "the baby" when I am taller than all my siblings does not make sense to me. When I was growing up, I was called "the Jerusalem baby" by some of the senior brethren at church because when my mother was expecting me, she went on a trip to Israel—a bold decision you might say. I can therefore say that I have been to the Holy Land (even though I didn't see anything because I was still in the womb).

I now live in Calgary, Alberta after I migrated there in 2014. I grew up in the Apostolic Faith as a member of Bethel United Church of Jesus Christ. I worshipped at No. 2 Gibson Road in Handsworth, Birmingham under the pastoral care of Bishop Sydney Alexander Dunn. I now worship at the Apostolic Ark Pentecostal Church of Calgary under the pastoral care of Bishop Horace Davey.

My Early Years

I learned to swear while in junior school—yes, junior school, but I only used this language at school. If my parents, who are strict Jamaican, ever heard me swear, I probably would not be alive today to write this book! Although I was baptized in Jesus name at the age of nine, I did not receive the gift of the Holy

Spirit until the age of sixteen. I attended an all-boys school, Handsworth Grammar School (HGS), between the ages of eleven and eighteen so I received the Holy Spirit towards the end of my secondary education. I later studied Accounting at the University of Wolverhampton and graduated with Honours in 2000. Unfortunately, I was unable to find employment upon graduation so I spent the next two years working for various employment agencies on temporary contracts until I obtained my first permanent role in 2003. I later worked for Ernst & Young LLP and Her Majesty's Revenue and Customs (HMRC) before I migrated to Canada.

A Double Life

Many people do not know this about me, but when I was in secondary school, I was a bit of a troublemaker. My parents raised me to be respectful and polite but I behaved differently when I was at school. I wanted to be popular at school. I guess I wanted to be liked, so I was a bit of a class clown at times. As a result of this, however, my early grades were poor. Due to my physical appearance, I could be quite intimidating when I wanted to be, but I was the recipient of the same treatment by older students at the school. I also experienced being bullied by pupils who were physically bigger than me, so I guess you could say I reaped what I had sown. I never took drugs or had pre-marital sex, but I did do others things of which I am not proud. I led a double life for several years, but my conscience would always trouble me. I knew what I was doing was wrong and I was fearful of the consequences if my parents found out. I guess you could say I knew the fear of my parents before I knew the fear of God! I always try to remember where I am coming from, and this helps me to remain grounded. It is easy to let people's praise get to your head so I always endeavour to give God the glory whenever praise is directed towards me. I know who I was and I know that it is only the grace of God why I have been able to accomplish anything positive in my life, including writing this book. It is only because of His Spirit that dwells within me why I am who I am today—all the glory belongs to Jesus Christ.

A New Creation

After I got baptised I gradually developed a desire for the Word of God. I would often stay up until the early hours of the morning reading the Bible in my bedroom. I would often read and memorize my favourite scriptures and make study notes. My favourite books growing up were 1 & 2 Timothy. I read them several times growing up and I still enjoy reading them today. I am, and always will be, a student of the Word of God.

There was a gap of seven years between when I was baptized in Jesus name and when I received the baptism of the Holy Spirit. During that seven-year period I went from one tarrying service to the next, not knowing for *whom* I was tarrying. I lost count of the number of times I fell asleep at the altar! On one occasion I was told that I had received the Holy Spirit, but I soon realized that I had not because there was no change in my lifestyle. In the Bible, the number seven is symbolic of completeness and perfection so maybe I had to wait until "I" was completely out of the way before I could receive what had been promised to me nearly two thousand years ago.

> *"For the promise is unto you, and to your children, and to all that are afar off, even as many as the* LORD *our God shall call." (Acts 2:39)*

The Night God Filled Me

At the beginning of every year Gibson Road church spends the first two weeks of the month seeking the Lord in fasting and prayer. In 1994, we also hosted a week of revival services. Our guest speaker that week was Dr. Colin Cawley from Toronto, Ontario. On the last night of the revival I decided I was not going to church. My brother asked me whether or not I was going and I told him "yes" (just so he would leave me alone), so he said that he would see me later. After he left my conscience started to bother me because I had lied to him. I knew I should have gone to church so I started to get dressed. I came out of my room and I started to make my way downstairs when I heard the telephone ring. I went back upstairs into my parent's room and picked up the phone but there was nobody on the other end. "Wrong number," I thought, so I put down the handset and made my way back downstairs. Then the phone rang again, so I went back into the room and picked up the handset. Again, there was nobody on the other end. Now, I know what you are thinking—I should have just pressed 1471 or *69 to get the number? I did not think of that at the time. I did get an eerie feeling at this point, but as it was getting late I just left the house and walked down the road to church.

The presence of God was in church that night. I honestly cannot remember the subject of the message that Dr. Cawley preached; it was over twenty years ago now, but I do remember going to the altar. It was not a service dedicated to seeking the infilling of the Holy Spirit but there I was at the altar seeking Him anyway. There was something different about this experience, this time I understood for *whom* I was seeking. Despite this understanding, it felt like I was making no progress. Looking back, I now realize I was struggling with my past. How could God fill me after all the things I had done? Elder George Peterkin was my spiritual "midwife" that evening and he encouraged me while I reached out to God in praise. I reached out to God for what seemed like an eternity but there came a point when I could sense that the service would soon be finishing. I knew I had not received the Holy Spirit and my chance to receive was slipping away. At this point I guess I began to get radical. I'll always remember what I said within myself.

"I am not leaving here God until you fill me!"

As soon as I said that it was as if something "clicked" in my spirit and I began to reach out to God like never before. It was not long after this that I was filled with the Holy Spirit. I began speaking in a heavenly language. I experienced the presence of God to the point that I had to be driven home. I remember being so thankful that God had filled me. Every time I reflected on where I was coming from, the Holy Spirit would bubble up within me and I would speak in tongues again. Nobody told me I received the Holy Spirit, He testified for Himself,

> "But when the Comforter is come, whom I will send unto you from the Father, even the Spirit of truth, which proceedeth from the Father, he shall testify of me:" (John 15:26)
>
> The Spirit itself beareth witness with our spirit, that we are the children of God:" (Rom. 8:15)

To this day, when I see Elder Peterkin, he often recounts the night I received the Holy Ghost, there is a special bond that exists between us.

The Holy Spirit Makes the Difference

Receiving the Holy Spirit has made a great difference in my life. My language and temperament changed. I stopped swearing and I began to hate even the sound of hearing other people swear. Before the Lord filled me with His Spirit I would hardly ever mention that I went to church much less talk about the Lord to my classmates. I remember an occasion when I was in my early teens, my mom gave my best friend and I a ride to school. While we were in the car she asked him whether he had ever been to church and if he would like to visit that Sunday. I sat in the front seat squirming as she was speaking to him. My classmates would often invite me to go to the cinema or out to a party but I knew deep inside that I could not go as my parents would not allow it. When they came back to school the following week, they would talk about which girl they were dating but when they asked me all I could say was that I went to church. It felt like they were having all the fun and I was just the "boring Christian." They had never seen me with a girlfriend or heard me talk about a girlfriend, so eventually some of them accused me of being gay. The truth is back then I wished I had a girlfriend, but I knew that my parents would not allow it. I envied them and I felt that I was missing out on something. I did not have a relationship with God to boast about—I *just* went to church. This began to change after I received the Holy Spirit. I found it easier to talk about the Lord and invite others to church. I would often get into discussions about God with my classmates and I was no longer ashamed or embarrassed to say I went to church. I remember going back to HGS sometime after I had completed my General Certificate in Secondary Education (GCSE) exams. While I was there I saw my old Business Studies teacher. In our Business Studies classes we would occasionally get into discussions about religion. There were Muslims, Sikhs, Hindus, and Atheists in my class, but I was the only Christian. While we reminisced about those discussions, he told me that one student (a Muslim) had visited the school and also talked about the discussions we used to have. Interestingly, he said to the teacher, "Shaun really knows his Bible." To think that even though he and other students criticized me at times for what I believed, he respected what I knew. Even though I did not know everything—and still do not— the little I did know helped me to defend the Gospel.

Young people are under pressure from school friends to do things that are contrary to the principles of the faith that we embrace. I have tried to fit in at school, I have tried to be liked by everybody and I have tried being the joker in the classroom. I did not realize that it was okay to stand out. If I knew then what I know now, I would have embraced my identity because I now understand who I am. I used to be ashamed growing up, but not anymore. I have been called various names; "Biblebasher" being the one I probably heard the most. I have been mocked and ridiculed by "friends," but I am not ashamed to be a child of God.

> *"For I am not ashamed of the gospel of Christ: for it is the power of God unto salvation to everyone that believeth; to the Jew first, and also to the Greek." (Rom. 1:16)*

Chapter 1

You Are Not Normal

"But ye are a chosen generation, a royal priesthood, an holy nation, a peculiar people; that ye should shew forth the praises of him who hath called you out of darkness into his marvelous light" (1 Pet. 2:9)

What Does It Mean to Be *Normal?*

The Oxford Dictionary and Thesaurus (1996) defines normal as *conforming to a standard, regular, usual, typical,* with the use of the following synonyms: *average, conventional, usual, ordinary, natural, conformist, etc.* (p.1034). Every day we see the world's view of normalcy. We see drinking, smoking, partying, dating, pre-marital sex, and so forth. We live in an era where people are not ashamed of who they are, in fact, they celebrate who they are. You dare not tell any of them that any aspect of their lifestyle is sinful as you may be labeled narrow-minded, old fashioned, or judgmental. We also live in an era of teen pregnancy, infidelity, suicide, drug abuse, mental instability, prostitution, witchcraft, and pornography. Homosexuality used to be a lifestyle that was practiced in secret, but now gay and lesbian couples not only have the right to get married, but they can adopt children as well. This is the new normal in 21st century society.

There is, however, another society that does not practice any of these and embraces a different set of values. Let us look at that society for a moment—what about the Church? Is there such a thing as a normal Christian? If there is, what does he or she look like? Can we even use the word normal to describe a Christian? Are there certain characteristics or behaviour patterns that we associate with Christianity? Let us look at the word Christian for a moment. What does it mean to be a Christian? The term Christian comes from the Greek word *Christianos,* which means "follower of Christ." The word *Christianos* appears three times in the Bible (all in the New Testament). It appears twice in the book of Acts and once in the Epistle of Peter. We are first introduced to *Christianos* in Acts chapter 11,

> *"And the disciples were called Christians first in Antioch." (Acts 11:26)*

The people gave the disciples this designation. Why? Could it be because the believers reminded them of the Man who ate with publicans and sinners, the Man who met a Samaritan woman at a well and left her *well* within, the Man who calmed the raging sea, the Man who healed the sick and raised the dead—the Man Christ Jesus? If this was one of the reasons, it raises another question, when people observe our conduct and behaviour of whom do we remind them? Do we remind them of the scribes, do we remind them of the self-righteous Pharisees and Sadducees or do we remind them of Jesus?

A Christian is someone who follows what Jesus said and did. Luke the Physician wrote to Theophilus about all that Jesus began to do and teach (Acts 1:1). I believe Jesus had a *show and tell* ministry; He led his disciples by example then taught his disciples what he had done and why. If you recall it was the disciples who asked Jesus to teach them how to pray

> *"And it came to pass, that, as he was praying in a certain place, when he ceased, one of his disciples said unto him, Lord, teach us to pray, as John also taught his disciples." (Luke 11:1)*

If they had never seen or heard Jesus pray they would not have asked him to teach them how. When the disciples could not cast out the demon from the man who had a lunatic son, they asked Jesus why they could not do it (Matt. 17:14–21). Our godly lifestyle should be the platform for us to make disciples of all men.

Discipleship 101

Jesus gave the requirements for anyone wanting to become one of his disciples,

> *"If any man will come after me, let him deny himself, take up his cross, and follow me." (Matt. 16:24)*

First of all I need to recognize that it is a choice. Jesus never forced anybody to become a disciple. He did however list three requirements.

1. Deny Himself

The life of a disciple is a life of self-denial, a denial of what my flesh wants or desires in favour of what God desires for me. I call self-denial the foundation stage of *Discipleship 101* and it is the most difficult. Once I have denied myself then taking up my cross (stage 2) and following Christ (stage 3) are easier. If I have not denied myself, then my cross becomes much heavier to bear because not only am I carrying the cross but I am also carrying the burden of my unbroken will.

2. Take Up His Cross

Once I have denied myself then the next stage is picking up my own cross. The cross denotes suffering because the person who carried his cross had an expectation that he would be crucified on it—this was the Roman method. The Apostle Peter wrote a few things about suffering in his epistles,

> *"But and if ye suffer for righteousness' sake, happy are ye: and be not afraid of their terror, neither be troubled." (1 Pet. 3:14)*

> *"For it is better, if the will of God be so, that ye suffer for well doing, than for evil doing." (1 Pet. 3:17)*

> *"Forasmuch then as Christ hath suffered for us in the flesh, arm yourselves likewise with the same mind: for he that hath suffered in the flesh hath ceased from sin;" (1 Pet. 4:1)*

As a disciple I should not only expect suffering but I should worship God in the midst of it,

> *"... if any man suffer as a Christian, let him not be ashamed: but let him glorify God ..." (1 Pet. 4:16)*

When suffering, we should always ask ourselves if we are suffering for Christ or because of sin. Solomon wrote that *the way of transgressors is hard* (Proverbs 13:15) so we should not be surprised if we are suffering because of our own wrongdoing.

If I desire to follow Jesus then I have to pick up my *own* cross; Jesus is not going to pick up my cross for me: He already carried His cross so I have to carry my own. You cannot carry my cross for me and I cannot carry your cross for you. The reason I have to carry my own cross is because that is the cross I will be crucified on. I believe the cross that Jesus carried was the heaviest of them all because He carried our sins.

> *"But [in fact] He has borne our griefs, And He has carried our sorrows and pains; Yet we [ignorantly] assumed that He was stricken, Struck down by*

God and degraded and humiliated [by Him]. But He was wounded for our transgressions, He was crushed for our wickedness [our sin, our injustice, our wrongdoing]; The punishment [required] for our well-being fell on Him, and by His stripes (wounds) we are healed. (Isa. 53:4–5 AMP)

So the songwriter Thomas Shepherd asked the following question,

Must Jesus bear the cross alone
And all the world go free?
No, there's a cross for everyone
And there's a cross for me.

Although I have to carry my own cross I can take comfort in knowing that because Jesus endured the cross I can endure it as well. When my cross feels too heavy to bear I can approach Him for help knowing that He understands how I feel.

"Looking unto Jesus the author and finisher of our faith; who for the joy that was set before him endured the cross, despising the shame, and is set down at the right hand of the throne of God." (Heb. 12:2)

"For we have not an high priest which cannot be touched with the feeling of our infirmities; but was in all points tempted like as we are, yet without sin. Let us therefore come boldly unto the throne of grace, that we may obtain mercy, and find grace to help in time of need." (Heb. 4:15–16)

3. Follow Me

Once I have denied myself and picked up my cross, then I can follow Him, The Greek word here is *Akoloutheo,* which means to follow the one who precedes, to join one as a disciple (Gk. *Mathetes*)—a pupil or learner.

> *"Take my yoke upon you, and learn of me; for I am meek and lowly in heart: and ye shall find rest unto your souls." (Matt. 11:29)*

A Normal Christian?

We have identified what the word normal means and we now have a definition of what the word Christian means. So what is a normal Christian? We may say normality for a Christian is church attendance; attendance at prayer meetings, fasting, tithing and putting money in the offering plate. We may say that brother or sister is "normal" or "saved." But is that all there is to being a normal Christian? Does doing all the *"church stuff"* mean we are saved? The Bible says,

> *"For by grace are ye saved through faith; and that not of yourselves: it is the gift of God: Not of works, lest any man should boast." (Eph. 2:8–9)*

If our definition is based solely on doing the *'church stuff,'* then salvation becomes works-based instead of a work of grace. If all I boast about is doing the *'church stuff,'* then be careful, as I may well be a Pharisee! The Bible reminds us of the story of a Pharisee and a publican who went to the temple to pray (Luke 18:10–14). The Pharisee came in his own righteousness while the publican came in repentant humility. Only one of them went home justified. I believe that we must endeavour to come to church as much as we can (Heb. 10:24–25) but we must always remember that going to church does not make us saved. Some of the biggest hypocrites attend church regularly. God desires a relationship with us more than doing the *'church stuff.'*

Go Beyond the Norm

If "normal Christianity" is defined as doing the "*church stuff*," then surely most of us would be "normal Christians." But there is a call to go beyond the norm and into an intimate relationship with God. Peter tells us that we are a **chosen generation** (1 Pet. 2:9). The Oxford Dictionary and Thesaurus (1996) says to be chosen means to be selected out of a great number (p. 450). At present, there are over seven billion people on this planet we call Earth, yet God (sovereignly) selected you and me out of 7 billion men and women to be his children. The Bible says,

> *"For many are called, but few are chosen."*
> *(Matt. 22:14)*

A universal call has been made; however, few have heard it with the inner ear, and even fewer have responded. We who have heard and answered the call are the *ecclesia* (the called-out ones). The Bible calls us kings and priests to God (Rev. 1:6). What a rags to riches story!

It Is Time to Fulfill Our Purpose

We need to understand that we only have a set amount of time on this planet to fulfil our divine purpose. Solomon writes

> *"To every thing there is a season, and a time to every purpose under the heaven:" (Eccles. 3:1)*

Milk has a purpose. We purchase milk from the grocery store or supermarket because it serves a purpose. Some of us use milk when making tea or coffee; some of us add it to our cereal when making breakfast while others drink milk on its own. Milk is good, it contains calcium, phosphorus, magnesium, protein, and other essential vitamins that help to maintain muscle, strengthen our bones and teeth, and release energy. But milk has a limited time to serve its purpose. In order for milk to be of benefit to us we have to open the container and consume it. If the milk is opened but left unused it will turn sour.

How many of us have become or will become sour because we not being used for His purpose?

> *"For ye are bought with a price: therefore glorify God in your body, and in your spirit, which are God's." (1 Cor. 6:20)*

Called to Serve Our Generation

You may never be called an Apostle, a Bishop, an Elder or an Evangelist but you have a call upon your life. Listen to what the Bible says of David

> *"For David, after he had **served** the purpose of God in **his** own **generation**, fell asleep and was buried among **his** fathers and experienced decay [in the grave];" (Acts 13:36 AMP)*

We live in a different generation to our forefathers. They did not have e-mail, airplanes, and social media but they used the ability that God gave them and they made themselves available to be used by God. They overcame various barriers (some racial, social and economic) in order to proclaim the undiluted Gospel to their generation. We are living in a different generation, our forefathers cannot reach this generation but we *can* and we have the opportunity to use the gifts, talents and resources at our disposal to communicate the Gospel message to our generation. Once we have served our purpose we can rest with our ancestors.

I Am a Priest

Do you realize that you are a priest? Not everybody could be a priest in the Old Testament. In fact, only those from the tribe of Levi were able to draw near to God, they had the responsibility for the Tabernacle of Moses and its holy vessels

> *"But thou shalt appoint the Levites over the tabernacle of testimony, and over all the vessels*

> *thereof, and over all things that belong to it: they shall bear the tabernacle, and all the vessels thereof; and they shall minister unto it, and shall encamp round about the tabernacle. And when the tabernacle setteth forward, the Levites shall take it down: and when the tabernacle is to be pitched, the Levites shall set it up: and the stranger that cometh nigh shall be put to death." (Num. 1:50–51)*

When the Lord made the covenant with the children of Israel, He stated that if they were obedient to Him, then they would be a 'kingdom of priests, a holy nation and a peculiar treasure' (see Exodus 19:6). Israel, however, forfeited this privilege through disobedience. I don't know about you, but I am not going to waste the chance I have been given to draw near, I am going to live as the priest God intended me to be, whether that is priest in my home or priest in the house of God. The priests in the Old Testament offered gifts and sacrifices to God. We, today, as spiritual priests, offer spiritual sacrifices,

> *"Ye also, as lively stones, are built up a spiritual house, an holy priesthood, to offer up spiritual sacrifices, acceptable to God by Jesus Christ." (1 Pet. 2:5)*

The Call to Sacrifice

We are called to offer a continual sacrifice of praise

> *"By him therefore let us offer the sacrifice of praise to God **continually**, that is, the fruit of our lips giving thanks to his name." (Heb. 13:15)*

We are also called as intercessors to stand in the gap for those who cannot reach God for themselves

> "And I sought for a man among them, that should make up the hedge, and stand in the gap before me for the land, that I should not destroy it: but I found none." (Ezek. 22:30)

It is a great responsibility being a priest. If the priest sinned, he had to offer a young bullock for a sin offering—if the congregation sinned a young bullock also had to be offered (compare Leviticus 4:5,11).

The Cost of Sacrifice

We cannot offer anything to God in the name of sacrifice, as we shall see in Chapter 5. King David was told to build an altar to the Lord on the threshingfloor of Araunah the Jebusite (2 Sam. 24:18). When David explained to Araunah why he wanted the threshing floor, Araunah offered to give David everything he needed to sacrifice to the Lord. Listen to David' response,

> "And the king said unto Araunah, Nay; but I will surely buy it of thee at a price: neither will I offer burnt offerings unto the LORD my God of that which doth cost me nothing. (2 Sam. 24:24)

How can we offer praise and worship that does not cost us anything? Why is it is called a "sacrifice of praise?" A sacrifice by definition will hurt; just imagine how Abraham felt when God told him to offer his only son Isaac on Mount Moriah? (Gen. 22:2). If we remember, Isaac was the son promised to Abraham when both he and Sarah were past the age of having children. Now the promise had finally arrived and God asked him to sacrifice the promise with no assurance that he would have more children. When he was about to go to sacrifice his son, he said to his servants,

> "I and the lad will go yonder and worship." (Gen. 21:5)

Could it be the reason we struggle to experience God's presence in worship is because no sacrifice has been or is being made? There was a woman who broke her alabaster box of ointment in order to anoint the feet of Jesus. The alabaster box was very expensive and so was the ointment that was stored within it. One of the disciples tried to put a price on it under the guise that it could have been put to better use.

> *"Why was not this ointment sold for three hundred pence, and given to the poor? (John 12:5)*

People (even church people) will be critical of how we worship and may even try to place a value on it. They may say "that is too much" or "It does not take all that," but we are not worshipping them so just break the box! Let us not be fearful or intimidated by who is around us, we paid the price for it—so break it. It may have been a year's wages in the spirit but break the box; nonetheless, no worship is wasted on Jesus!

I Am Royalty

Not only am I a priest but I am royalty as well. My Daddy is the King of kings and the LORD of Lords (1 Tim. 6:15) so I am of royal descent. God does not have any broke, lame, or poor sons. John wrote that we are kings (Rev. 1:8) so we have all right to prosper (spiritually and otherwise) while we are walking in the will of God. Young people, I want to encourage you not to settle for minimum wage, set your sights and goals higher. In his book *Rich Dad, Poor Dad* (2011), American businessman Robert Kiyosaki used the word "job" as an acronym for *Just Over Broke* (p.160). Young people, we should be thinking of owning our own businesses, not working our entire life for ungodly men and women who have no covenant relationship with Jehovah-God. I believe God has put ideas in us, creativity and intellect, vision and ability. Some of us are authors, actors, musicians, songwriters, scriptwriters and so forth. We should not settle for being an *employee* living from paycheck to paycheck when we can be an **employer**. We should tap into our God given ability and strive to excel and bring glory to God in whatever sphere he has called us to be in. We should be striving to own our own property not struggling to pay rent. Why? We serve Jehovah (the Self-Existent One) who is also the El-Shaddai (the God of more than enough). Jesus said that He came that we might have life more abundantly (John 10:10). The word abundantly speaks of *super*-abundance, an overflowing of not just spiritual blessings and experiences but also of material blessings. Prosperity is promised to us if we walk in obedience to the Word of God (read Deut. 28:1–14).

I have heard a lot of criticism over the years directed at so called "prosperity preachers" and I have also heard many people try to justify being poor. Some Christians say, "When we were poor we served God better" and to a certain extent I understand the statement. But we must also understand we are entitled to wealth because we are kings. The Lord warned the children of Israel

> *"But thou shalt remember the Lord thy God: for it is he that giveth thee power to get wealth, that he may establish his covenant which he sware unto thy fathers, as it is this day." (Deut. 8:18)*

If provision has been made for us to have wealth so that God's kingdom can be established in the earth why would we prefer to live in poverty? God does not have a problem with us having money as long as money does not have us. God has given us the power to get wealth not so we can dress in designer clothes, live in extravagant houses, and drive flashy cars but so we can spread the gospel message to a dying world. We live in an era of air travel and it is going to take wealth to travel to the regions beyond to preach the gospel. I agree that some of these "*prosperity preachers*" are living in luxury with private jets, huge mansions and expensive cars, all while many of the people that they shepherd are struggling financially. These hirelings may be fleecing the sheep financially but leave them to God, the wheat will be separated from the tares when harvest comes

> *"Let both grow together until the harvest: and in the time of harvest I will say to the reapers, Gather ye together first the tares, and bind them in bundles to burn them: but gather the wheat into my barn." (Matt. 13:30)*

I Am a Steward

God has made us stewards over His goods so why would He give us more if we only use what He has given for ourselves and not for His purposes? Could it be that the reason we are experiencing lack is because we have been bad stewards of the goods that God has already given to us? Instead of sowing into the kingdom, we keep what we have for ourselves. When we should be a blessing to someone we hold onto the blessing and then we wonder why we are not prospering. I refuse to live below my privileges, I am going to be obedient to the Word of God and receive everything that His Word says is for me. I pray you do the same.

Chapter 2

The Call to Be Different

There is a difference between the world and us. Whether we choose to accept it or not, there is difference between the world and us. There are things that have happened in our lives that were meant to and should have killed us, but we are still alive. There are people that have not been through half of what we have been through in our lives yet they are not here to tell their story.

In 1994, I sat my GCSE exams. This was a very stressful time for me, although no one would have known it just by looking at me. By the grace of God and the prayers of the saints, I passed all of my exams. I remember when I went to collect my results from school; I met a fellow student who said to me that he and another student had taken prescription medication in order to cope with the stress. I was completely oblivious to the lengths some people will go to in order to cope with stress. We all sat the same exams but while prayer helped me cope with the pressure, others had to rely on prescription medication to get through. This is not just a coincidence or some new phenomenon, this has been happening since Biblical times. When the children of Israel were in Egyptian bondage, Jehovah afflicted the Egyptians with various plagues so that Pharaoh would let His people go. The last plague was the death of the firstborn. While all the firstborn in Egypt would die the Lord said,

> "But against any of the children of Israel shall not a dog move his tongue, against man or beast: that ye may know how that the Lord doth put a difference between the Egyptians and Israel." (Exod. 11:7)

We Are Different

What does it mean to be different? If someone were to describe you as "different," what thoughts or images would come to mind? If your best friend described you as "different" would you be offended? Being different often has a derogatory meaning. It can mean weird, odd, eccentric, and so forth. The Oxford Dictionary and Thesaurus defines the word different as being *distinguishable in nature, unusual, new, not the same as, separate*—that is exactly what you are, child of God. It is about time the world desires to be like the church instead of the church desiring to be like the world. God does not want His children to imitate the world but He wants His children to set the standard for the world. We are supposed to be the trendsetters.

Please, Pass the Salt

The world is crying out for *more salt!* Jesus said,

> "Ye are the salt of the earth: but if the salt have lost his savour, wherewith shall it be salted? it is thenceforth good for nothing, but to be cast out, and to be trodden under foot of men." (Matt. 5:13)

Salt has the ability to change any environment in which it is placed. It is time for us to be sprinkled out at school, at university, in our workplaces, in our homes and in our communities. God has placed us in strategic positions for a reason—it is not even about us, it is about Him. We are there for a purpose— *to* *aff*ect someone's life. Salt affects everything with which it comes in contact. Why is salt is put on the road when it snows, sometimes even before the snow falls? Salt affects the snow by lowering the freezing point of water. When it is sprinkled on ice, it makes a brine with the film of surface water, which lowers the freezing point and starts melting the ice that the brine is in contact with. Also, salt prevents ice from forming because salt water freezes at a lower temperature than pure water, so the salt helps to prevent the falling snow from freezing. Some of us have been sprinkled like salt into the life of others to melt their icy hearts. Some of us have been sent ahead like a gritter or salt truck to prevent situations from becoming treacherous.

The Church Outside The Four Walls

We may never preach a message from a pulpit or sing a solo on a choir but we are salt **wherever** we are. In fact, do we realize we can affect more people *outside* the four walls of our church building than we can inside? In fact, when we think about it, we spend the majority of our time outside of the four walls of our local assembly. My wife is a Maths teacher so let us do some Maths to illustrate my point. There are 168 hours in every week. If I attend church three times a week, say on Sunday, Wednesday, and Friday and spend two hours per service, I would have spent 6 hours per week in church, which is less than 4% of my week. That means the greater part of my week (more than 96% or 162 hours) is spent **outside** of the church building, interacting with people who I may never see *inside* the church building. We are able to positively affect someone's life without them even coming inside the physical building because we **are** the church.

But We Want To Be Like Everyone Else

The problem that many of us face today is that we do not like being different. This is not a new problem. When Samuel's sons Joel and Abiah failed to follow in their father's godly footsteps the elders of Israel called Samuel and asked for a king to judge them like the other nations (1 Sam. 8:5). This request upset Samuel but when he went to the Lord in prayer the Lord explained that Israel had rejected Him as their king. Samuel warned Israel the kind of king they would get, but Israel's response was,

> *"Nay; but we will have a king over us; that we also may be like all the nations; and that our king may judge us, and go out before us, and fight our battles." (1 Sam. 8:19–20)*

The Israelites had now forgotten who brought them to where they were. Here are just a few examples of what Jehovah (the King of kings) had done
- Opened up the Red Sea so their forefathers could cross over on dry land (Exod. 14)
- Turned the bitter waters of Marah sweet and provided quails and manna in the wilderness (Exod. 15:23–26; 16:10–20)
- Prevented their ancestors' feet from swelling while wandering for 40 years in the wilderness (Deut. 6:4)
- Delivered them from Sihon, king of Heshbon and Og king of Bashan (Num. 21:21–26; 33–35)
- Turned the curse of Balak into a blessing (Num. 22–24)

Israel wanted a finite king to fight their battles for them even though Jehovah God was infinite and undefeated in battle. This generation had not witnessed the miraculous power of God for itself so it took for granted how they got to where they were.

Is History Repeating Itself?

The following quote is often attributed to George Santayana, a Spanish philosopher. It says,

> *"Those who do not learn from history are doomed to repeat it."*

Many young people today are experiencing the same issues the children of Israel encountered—they want to be like everyone else. Some have one foot in church and the other foot in the world. Some desire a relationship with God, but also want to be free to do as they please as well. They may sing on the choir, but they are with someone in the world at the same time. Some may attend church on a Sunday but are at the club during the week. Some enjoy the praise and worship and the high of being in the presence of God but they are drawn to the things of the world as well. Brothers and sisters we cannot have both. What we fail to realize is that everything we *need* is in God.

A Word To My Younger Brothers

Some of us behave as though we have a reputation to protect. It is as though if we do not have a girlfriend then we are not "cool." Brothers, if we are more concerned about our reputation then maybe we have an issue with pride! Jesus was not concerned about his reputation yet He was God robed in flesh. I do not need to "check"; date, or "link" with a girl to prove who I am. Our manliness is not determined by the number of girlfriends or sexual conquests we have. Hell is *hot*, but being set apart is *cool*. A young man who is a virgin is not normal in the 21st century. I know what it means to be ridiculed for not having a girlfriend. Some "friends" of mine even questioned my sexuality because I did not have a girlfriend like they did, but at the end of the day their opinion was not important to me. Brothers, when are we going to recognize the value of our sisters? Our sisters in Christ are to be valued, protected, and treated with respect—not used for sexual gratification. We have a great responsibility to ensure they are not wounded or violated. Remember your body is the temple of the Holy Ghost (1 Cor. 6:19).

Paul writes,

> *"If any man defile the temple of God, him shall God destroy; for the temple of God is holy, which temple ye are." (1 Cor. 3:17)*

If I am promiscuous, I am defiling two temples (my own and my sister's). Growing up I have often heard sisters being encouraged to respect themselves but brothers we need to respect ourselves as well. We are men of God, priests, leaders, soldiers, warriors for the Lord. We need to have respect not just for who we are right now, but for who God has called us to be. Brothers, let us be careful what we say to our sisters in Christ because our words can have a powerful effect on them. I have heard it said that women respond more to auditory stimuli than visual (i.e. what they hear more than what they see); therefore, we can build a sister's hopes and expectations with our words. Let us endeavour to build our sister's spirit with words of edification, not words of flattery or seduction. How many arguments and disputes have arisen because a silver-tongued devil has given several young sisters his *undivided attention?* This "devil" has no intention of marrying any of them, but he is talking exclusively to each one and, consequently, they are all expecting marriage because he is using the right words, like the reality TV series "The Bachelor." Eventually, at least one sister is left hurt, heartbroken, and disappointed with no trust in men. What happens when the Lord sends her a faithful brother to be her husband, but she is still carrying the baggage of failed expectations? Now imagine that *you* are that faithful brother who has to deal with the consequences. Imagine if the girl with the broken heart was your daughter or your sister. How much more patience, love, and understanding will have to be shown in order to rebuild her trust, all because someone used his words to give her false hope? Brothers, make a vow not to injure your sister in Christ with your words.

A Word to My Younger Sisters

I am asking you to protect your brothers in Christ and encourage them to study the Word. Encourage them to seek the face of the Lord and to become the leader and priest that God wants them to be. While women are influenced by auditory stimuli, men are influenced by visual stimuli so protect your brother by dressing appropriately. You do not need to wear a burka[1]; I truly believe if you have the Holy Spirit alive and reigning in you, He will teach you what is appropriate to wear. Respect your body and respect your chastity; holiness is still cool. We live in an era where sex sells virtually everything. It is on the television, on billboards, in magazines and online. Sex before marriage is the norm but so is teen pregnancy and sexually transmitted diseases (STDs). Sisters, you do not need to look outside of church for your husband, if it is God's will for you to get married, the man He has ordained for you is in the church. I can only imagine how hard it must be to wait for a brother to show an interest in you, let alone ask for your hand in marriage, but I am pleading with you not to go out into the world to seek a husband. Sisters, do not throw away your chastity by having pre-marital sex. All you are doing is defiling yourself while the enemy is laughing at how easy it is to deceive you. How many powerful young sisters have fallen because a man seduced her then left her (literally) holding the baby. How many powerful young men have fallen because they could not resist the charms of a woman? How many young people in church are having sex and coming to church as though nothing is wrong? Just because God has not exposed what happened does not mean that He has not seen it. If you have sinned, I encourage you to confess your sin to God and repent. The Bible says,

> "If we confess our sins, he is faithful and just to forgive us our sins, and to cleanse us from all unrighteousness." (1 John 1:9)

No matter what you have done, God is able to restore you to fellowship with Him.

The Grass Is Not Greener Over There

Grass vs. Astroturf

The world tries to show us that the grass on the other side of the fence is greener but I always remember a close friend and brother once said to me, "the reason the grass looks greener is because it is *Astroturf!*" Astroturf is *synthetic,* it is *artificial,* and it is *not* real grass. It is a cheap alternative. What the world is offering looks like real joy but it is merely a cheap substitute; it may even look like real peace but it's not real peace. It's *synthetic*—there is no substance to it; it is like comparing a real apple or banana to a plastic one. Both may look the same on the outside, but try taking a bite out of a real apple then try to bite the plastic apple and you will see there is a significant difference between the two—ok, don't try it, just take my word for it. Jesus said,

> "These things have I spoken unto you, that my joy might remain in you, and that your joy might be full." (John 15:11)

The world is happy one day and sad the next because their happiness is based on happenings (life events). The joy that Jesus gives is not linked to positive or negative life events but is linked to His abiding presence.

> *"Thou wilt shew me the path of life: in thy presence is fulness of joy; at thy right hand there are pleasures for evermore." (Ps. 16:11)*

> *"And I will pray the Father, and he shall give you another Comforter, that he may abide with you for ever" (John 14:16).*

The peace the world offers is not true peace. Jesus gives true peace (Heb. *Shalom*—completeness, soundness) in the midst of the chaos of life, a peace that passes all understanding (Philippians 4:7). It is a peace that cannot be comprehended by the world because they have no relationship with Him. Look what David wrote in the Psalms,

> *"Great peace have they which love thy law: and nothing shall offend them." (Ps. 119:165)*

This peace is so great that no matter the circumstance or life events we face, it will not cause us to stumble or be a stumbling block in our way.

What I Don't Know Will Destroy Me

The problem that we face is that too many of us are ignorant of the Word of God. A popular phrase in the world is "ignorance is bliss." Another one states, "What you do not know cannot hurt you." The Lord told the prophet Hosea that His people were destroyed because of a lack of knowledge (Hos. 4:6). The Lord told the prophet Isaiah that His people went into captivity because they had no knowledge (Isaiah 5:13). Captivity is the state of being a slave or being imprisoned and it is a sad commentary of our generation that many of us are imprisoned in our own minds because we have no knowledge (Heb. *Da'ath*—understanding) of the Word of God. We are living in the most advanced era in human history, an era where we are able to access multiple versions of the Bible. We have access to teaching, preaching, music, and worship services on

CD, DVD and live streaming. There are many tools to study the Bible; Concordances, Lexicons, Study Bibles, Bible Maps, Atlases, Bible Dictionaries, Commentaries et cetera. The question is, are we making use of the abundance of resources at our disposal. How many of us are spending time in the Word?

Theologians know about Him, only true Christians know Him.

Ask yourself this question, when was the last time I spent an hour in the Word because I wanted to know Him? Is the only time I read the Bible when I am asked to do or say something in church? Do I study to know *about* Him or do I study to *know* Him. Instead of spending time in the Word and in the presence of God, many of us, especially our young people are spending time on the phone, on social media, playing video games, or watching TV. The Lord told Hosea,

> "because thou hast rejected knowledge, I will also reject thee, that thou shalt be no priest to me: seeing thou hast forgotten the law of thy God, I will also forget thy children." (Hos. 4:6)

If we reject knowledge, God will in turn reject us as being His priests. If we are no longer His priests, we forfeit the privilege of being in His presence, which basically means we will die spiritually.

Samson Was Called to Be Different

To end this chapter, I want to take a look at the life of Samson as an example of someone who was called to be different. Samson's path was chosen for him before he was even conceived. Samson's mother was barren but the angel of the Lord appeared to her and told her that she was going to have a son who would be a deliverer. She was given an insight into his destiny and instructions on how he should be raised.

> *"For, lo, thou shalt conceive, and bear a son; and no razor shall come on his head: for the child shall be a Nazarite unto God from the womb: and he shall begin to deliver Israel out of the hand of the Philistines. (Judg. 13:5)*
>
> *"Behold, thou shalt conceive, and bear a son; and now drink no wine nor strong drink, neither eat any unclean thing: for the child shall be a Nazarite to God from the womb to the day of his death." (Judg. 13:7)*

There was something different about Samson; the fact that he was a Nazarite was not uncommon as anyone (male or female) could make a Nazarite vow (see Numbers 6:1). The unusual part is that Samson never personally made the decision to become a Nazarite; God made the decision sovereignly that he would be a Nazarite—Samson had no choice in the matter. Before he came out of the womb he was separated unto God, before he uttered his first words or took his first steps he was already under the vow of a Nazarite; he was *born* different! Have you ever felt like you did not have a choice about who God has called you to be or what He has called you to do? Some things in your life are out of your control. Imagine for a moment how Samson might have felt interacting with his friends growing up? Maybe his friends had 'normal' hair while his hair was allowed to grow; maybe he was teased or mocked because his hair was different? As he grew older, he may have witnessed his friends drinking alcohol but he could not because he was different. Samson was blessed and as he grew the Spirit of the Lord started to manifest in his life (Judg. 13:24–25). I want to highlight three relationships that Samson had with women, each of which resulted in trouble for Samson, the last of which would ultimately cost him his life.

Relationship Number 1

The first relationship began when Samson went down to Timnath (in Philistia) and saw a Philistine woman. He asked his parents to arrange for him to marry this woman but his parents pleaded with him to look for a wife from among his own people. The Philistines were enemies of Israel. We may have read or heard the phrase *'uncircumcised Philistines'* referring to the fact that they had no covenant relationship with Jehovah God. Samson had his heart set on marrying this woman. He told his parents,

> *"Get her for me. She is the right one for me"*
> *(Judg. 14:3 NIV)*

Samson wanted to marry an idol worshipper, which was forbidden under Mosaic Law (Deut. 7:3). How many of us are looking for relationships with the uncircumcised in *heart*? How many are already in relationships with unbelievers? Relationships with the unsaved rarely end well for the child of God. The Lord, through the prophet Amos, asked a question,

> *"can two walk together except they be agreed?"*
> *(Amos 3:3)*

A Christian and an unbeliever are essentially walking in different directions. When one wants to go to church the other wants to stay at home and watch TV. When one wants to go to the bingo or to the club, the other wants to pray or study the Word—they are heading in different directions. Paul encouraged the believers in Corinth not to be unequally yoked together with unbelievers because righteousness and unrighteousness cannot fellowship together (see 2 Corinthians 6:14). Although the Lord ultimately used the situation to accomplish His divine purpose, I do not believe the Lord was pleased with Samson's actions. Samson thought everything was okay because the Spirit of the Lord continued to come mightily upon him (Judg. 14:6; 15:14). Samson later went back to Timnath with his parents. While in the vineyards in Timnath[2], Samson killed a lion that attacked him but he did not tell his parents about the incident. When he later returned to Timnath to marry the woman, he saw the carcass of the lion and a swarm of bees and honey in the carcass (verse 8). He took the honey from the carcass, ate some and gave some to his parents, again without telling them where it came from (verse 9). Samson had broken his vow by touching the carcass. Now the Mosaic Law provided a remedy if an individual violated his Nazarite vow,

> *"And if any man die very suddenly by him, and he hath defiled the head of his consecration; then he shall shave his head in the day of his cleansing, on the seventh day shall he shave it. And on the eighth day he shall bring two turtles, or two young pigeons, to the priest, to the door of the tabernacle of the congregation: And the priest shall offer the one for a sin offering, and the other for a burnt offering, and make an atonement for him, for that he sinned by the dead, and shall hallow his head that same day." (Num. 6:9–11)*

Samson did not shave his head or bring the necessary sacrifices to the priest to make atonement for himself—he continued in violation of his consecration. Samson married the Philistine woman who manipulated him into giving her the answer to the riddle he had posed to the men of the city (Judg. 15:16–17). Samson's wife was later given to his companion (Judg. 15:2) and their relationship ended when both her and her father were burned to death (Judg. 15:6).

Relationship Number 2

Samson's next 'relationship' was with a harlot (a prostitute).

> *"Then went Samson to Gaza, and saw there an harlot, and went in unto her." (Judg. 16:1)*

While he was there the people of Gaza found out and they surrounded the city by night (intending to kill him in the morning). Samson got up at midnight and escaped out of the city by carrying the doors and doorposts of the city gates on his shoulders. Despite this escape, Samson did not change his ways; he still thought everything was okay because the Spirit of the Lord was still moving upon him. How many times have we been in trouble of our own making but God delivered us? Just because we made it out of the situation alive does not mean that God was or is pleased with our actions. We need to repent and clean up our act before it is too late.

Relationship Number 3

Samson's final recorded relationship was the one that brought about his downfall. When I was reading about Delilah I noticed that the Bible does not say a great deal about her, so I referred to other sources to learn a bit more about her. The Unger's Bible Dictionary (1957) uses the word *coquette* to describe Delilah (p. 297). Webster (2014) defines a *coquette* as a woman who endeavours without sincere affection to gain the attention and admiration of men (p. 276). Unger's Bible Dictionary (1957) also uses the word *courtesan* to describe Delilah (p. 276). Webster (2014) says a courtesan is a prostitute with a courtly, wealthy or upper-class clientele (p. 287).

Delilah's Valley

Delilah lived in the Valley of Sorek. The map below shows the location of the Valley of Sorek; as you can see it was situated between the territory of the Israelites and the Philistines.

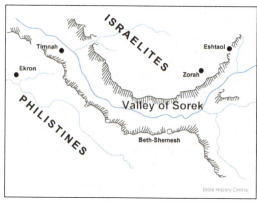

The Valley of Sorek

In order to get to the Valley of Sorek, Samson had to leave Israelite territory. But if you look closely Samson could be in Sorek but not yet in Philistine territory. In the Valley of Sorek he was neither in Israel nor in Philistia, he was neither in the Israelite camp nor in the Philistine camp, he was between two identities (being fully in Israel and being fully in Philistia) and in a place of uncertainty. Delilah can only reach you when you are in her valley. In the same way some of us are in the valley of indecision, we are not fully in church but we are not fully in the world either—we are in the valley of Sorek, which is a dangerous place to be.

She Does Not Feel the Same Way

The Bible specifically states that Samson loved Delilah (Judg. 16:4) so we can infer that there may have been a soul-tie[3] between them. Notice the Bible does not say anything to suggest that Delilah loved Samson. I believe that the soul-tie that existed between Samson and Delilah was so strong that it blinded Samson from seeing Delilah's agenda and ultimately caused him to reveal the secret of his strength. Delilah was not subtle about her intentions toward Samson. She spelt out exactly what she intended to do to him.

> "Tell me, I pray thee, wherein thy great strength lieth, and wherewith thou mightest be bound to afflict thee." (Judg. 16:6)

> "Now tell me, I pray thee, wherewith thou mightest be bound." (verse.10)

> "Tell me wherewith thou mightest be bound." (verse.13)

If someone kept asking what he or she needed to do to me to cause me the most harm I would want to know why, wouldn't you? Samson could not see her end game because he was 'in love' with her. The more she asked Samson about the source of his strength, the closer she got to revealing his secret.

> "If they bind me with seven green withs that were never dried" (verse. 7)

> "If they bind me fast with new ropes that never were occupied" (verse.11)

> "If thou weavest the seven locks of my head with the web" (verse.13)

Delilah eventually realized that Samson would not immediately divulge his secret so she changed her strategy and began to question Samson's love for her,

> "How canst thou say, I love thee, when thine heart is not with me? Thou hast mocked me these three times, and hast not told me wherein thy great strength lieth." (verse.15)

The enemy will continue pressing until he finds our area of weakness, once we succumb to his tactics once, he then knows which buttons to press and he can get to us at any time.

Samson had previously been manipulated (Judg. 14:16–17) so the enemy knew that all it would take was consistent pressure and he would eventually reveal his secret. The Bible says that Delilah pressed him *daily* until his soul was vexed unto death (vs.16). Delilah used Samson's "love" for her to manipulate him into revealing his secret. Delilah was not interested in Samson; she did not love or even care about him. Delilah was an opportunist. Delilah could be bought because Delilah has a price!

> *"Entice him, and see wherein his great strength lieth ... and we will give thee every one of us eleven hundred pieces of silver." (Judg. 16:5)*

I call Delilah the *designated assassin* of every consecrated man (or woman) of God. When Samson eventually told Delilah all his heart she immediately called the Philistines (who were lying in wait) to capture him. Delilah made Samson sleep in her lap. While Samson was sleeping comfortably in Delilah's lap she called an attendant to shave the locks of his hair, then she started to afflict him. We need to recognize that by this time Samson was already spiritually unconscious so he could not understand what was being done to him. While Samson was dreaming the enemy was shaving his hair.

The question is, whose lap am I lying in? What is the enemy doing to me while I am ignorant to his devices? Who is my Delilah? The Delilah in the Bible was a woman but we need to understand that Delilah could be a man. Does he (or she) *really* love me or is there an ulterior motive? Many Christians have lost their anointing while they slept in the enemy's lap. Some have lost their commitment to the Lord while others have lost their zeal and enthusiasm. Samson was never the same again. When he woke up he had no strength and was easily captured by the Philistines. There was no miraculous escape this time. In fact, he did not even realize that the Spirit of the Lord had departed from him (Judg. 16:20). He felt that he could just shake himself like all the other times and he would experience the same power he experienced in the past. Am I living off past experiences or my present relationship with God? Some Christians are judging their present condition based how God used them 5 or even 10 years ago.

Samson's eyes were taken out (Prov. 29:18) but he lost his vision before his eyes were removed. After his capture, the Philistines brought him to their place of worship and made a mockery of him, which is exactly what the enemy will do if he catches us. We know that Samson's hair began to grow again but in the end we cannot say with absolute certainty that Samson was saved because he took his own life (read Judg. 16:25–30 and Rev. 21:8). The life of Samson teaches that fruit (not gifts) is the only true barometer of a person's life. It does not matter how much we speak in tongues or how mightily the Lord uses us, if we do not live consecrated lives, we will end up bound with no vision and no hope for the future.

The children of Israel were *different* but they wanted to be like everyone else. Samson was *born* different, but he had one foot in Israel (the church) and the other foot in Philistia (the world). The question is: am I going to embrace being different or am I going to try to be like everyone else?

Chapter 3

It Is OK to Stand Out

"And be not conformed to this world; but be ye transformed by the renewing of your mind, that ye may proved what is that good, and acceptable and perfect will of God." (Rom. 12:2)

People today are not ashamed or afraid to be different. Some dye their hair bright colors (orange, purple, blonde) while others dye it black. Some allow their hair to grow longer than usual while others shave it off completely. Some people wear make up or jewelry while others get piercings or tattoos on various parts of their body. Some people stand out because of the way they think or express their opinion. It may be they express very liberal views on issues like abortion, gay rights, or the legalization of certain drugs like marijuana or cannabis. Others may be ultra conservative on the same issues. Because of the various ways that people express their identity we may feel pressured to try to "fit in" or "be liked" by the people we associate with.

What Does It Mean to Conform?

According to the Oxford Dictionary and Thesaurus (1996) to conform means to '*comply with rules or general custom*' (p.1034). The Greek word translated 'conform' in Romans

12:2 is *suschematizo*. It conveys the idea of conforming one's self (i.e. one's mind and character) to another's pattern, to fashion one's self according to. Today, we are under pressure to fashion ourselves according to the pattern of the world. The pressure we face is oftentimes so subtle that we can find ourselves conforming without even realizing it. But we have not been called to fashion ourselves after the world, instead we have been called to be transformed (Gk. *metamorphousthe*) by the renewing of our minds.

I believe the Lord showed me something many years ago while I was meditating on Him. The words "don't try to fit in" came to me. As I was meditating, I pictured two jigsaw puzzles, one representing the world and one representing the church. As sinners, we were in the world's "jigsaw puzzle" and we fitted in. Many of us may have sinned without regret and had no thought of changing. But one day we realized that there was something missing in our lives. Some of us tried various things, looking for something or someone that could fill the God-sized void that existed within. One day *something* or *someone* led us to go to church.

> *"No man can come to me, except the Father which hath sent me draw him: and I will raise him up at the last day." (John 6:44)*

Eventually we decided to give our lives to Jesus Christ. When we repented of our sins this symbolized our death. When someone dies naturally, they are buried (in a grave). In the same way repentance represents death to our old lifestyle. We were then buried in the (watery) grave called the baptismal pool (Rom. 6:4). When the minister brought us up out of the pool our new life in Christ began—we became a new creation

> *"Therefore if any man be in Christ, he is a new creature: old things are passed away; behold, all things are become new." (2 Cor. 5:17)*

We were taken out of the world's "jigsaw puzzle," reshaped, remolded and placed into another jigsaw puzzle—the church. After receiving the gift of the Holy Spirit, we began to grow spiritually as we build our new relationship with the Lord.

I Belong to God Now

The problem (if we can call it a problem) that many Christians face is that we have outgrown the things of the world so we do not fit into the world's puzzle anymore. When we were in the world we had a worldly mentality but now we are saved everything has changed, our taste buds have changed (or should have), our desires have changed (or should have). The things that used to interest us no longer appeal to us and this can create a conflict within us. People may even have asked if something is wrong with us because we are no longer interested in going to the same places that we used to go to or doing the things they are accustomed to us doing—we simply do not fit in anymore. What God showed me is that we are *not supposed* to fit in with the world anymore. If we try and fit into the world system, we will encounter problems. Have you ever seen a child try to fit a jigsaw piece from one puzzle into another one? Or maybe you have watched a child with building blocks try to put a square block into a round whole (or you have done it yourself). Look at the picture below.

As you can see from the image, the rectangular block *does not* fit into the round hole no matter how hard you try—it is different from the rest of the blocks. The problem with trying to fit the rectangular block into the round hole is not so much the amount of time and effort and frustration of forcing the fit, but that you end up damaging the block. Look what happens (see picture below) when you try to force the square block into the round whole (using a hammer).

As you can see the square block now fits into the round whole but the block is damaged. This is what happens when we try too hard to fit in the world. The world breaks us down, chips away our joy, cracks our peace, and it destroys our patience and our love. This is also what happens during the backsliding process. A child of God who backslides does not do so overnight. Backsliding is a process that happens gradually and may be happening while I am still coming to church.

Here are some of the tell tale signs of backsliding:

A. I stop praying and reading the Word.

In the natural it is impossible to have a healthy relationship without communication. The more I speak with you the more I know about you; I will eventually get to know what your likes or dislikes are. When I stop praying and reading the Word of God, I cut off my communication with my Heavenly Father. I no longer know what God is saying therefore I cannot do what pleases Him. The Bible is the will and the mind of God. In the natural, if I am an executor in a will, it would really be advisable to find out what the will says—after all I have to carry out the wishes of the testator. If I do not know what God's word is saying then how do I know whether I am pleasing him and doing his will?

B. My commitment to fasting gradually decreases until I stop fasting completely.

This means that my flesh (sinful nature) is no longer under subjection so I am less likely to yield my will to the Spirit of God. When I fast, I deny myself of what my flesh wants (food) so that I can feed my spirit man. If I feed my spirit man and starve my flesh, then I will grow spiritually.

C. I gradually stop going to church.

When I stop fasting, praying and reading the Word, my desire for the things of God will begin to wane which includes going to church. This means I am missing out on the spoken Word (see John 6:63) as well as the fellowship of the saints (see Ps. 133:1–3; Prov. 27:17). Many of us fail to appreciate the importance of the assembling of the saints together which is dangerous. The writer of the book of Hebrews basically encouraged the brethren not to forsake (abandon) coming to church.

> *"not forsaking our meeting together [as believers for worship and instruction], as is the habit of some, but encouraging one another; and all the more [faithfully] as you see the day [of Christ's return] approaching." (Heb. 10:25 AMP)*

When I stop coming to church I leave myself open to the attack of the enemy, who will try to isolate me (as a sheep) from the rest of the church (flock). He will plant seeds in my mind telling me that nobody loves me. He will try to weaken my defenses so I start to believe there is no love in the church, that nobody cares about me and I am all by myself. If he is successful I will miss church for weeks at a time until eventually I stop going.

Notice the first two signs of backsliding are not visible to the *"natural eye."* You cannot usually tell by looking at me whether or not I read the Bible at home or whether or not I fast or pray regularly. If I know how to "talk the talk" and use certain clichés, I may be able convince someone that I am okay, even when I might be dying spiritually. There is a saying attributed to Abraham Lincoln,

> "You can fool all the people some of the time, and some of the people all the time, but you cannot fool all the people all the time."

I know from experience that God will send someone to speak to us so that we do not die. Why? Because He loves us.

We Have All Done It

I am sure many Christians can relate to having backslidden at some point during their walk with the Lord—I know I can relate so I know at least one of the signs personally. Some of us, like the prodigal son have recognized that we have fallen from our steadfastness and through true repentance and God's grace and mercy we were able to get back on track. Others however, have gradually drifted away, failing to recognize the signs. The scary fact is that some of us have backslidden but we are *still* coming to church. We are in the building but we are far away from God. When a person backslides, he or she eventually starts to decay spiritually. He or she loses the joy he or she had before; the enthusiasm he or she had for the things of God, the godly characteristics are no longer there, and even his or her countenance begins the change.

Depreciation

Did you know that God uses the natural to show us the spiritual? When I was at university studying for my Accounting degree I learned about "depreciation." The Oxford Dictionary and Thesaurus (1996) says the word depreciation means to "*diminish in value*" (p. 300). A business that owns assets (buildings, land, equipment, etc.) will reduce the value of them over their useful life to take account of how much of the asset has been used over the accounting year. I believe this has a spiritual application. When we were in the world we were owned by the devil. He used us to do what pleased him. While we belonged to him we were depreciating *(losing value)*. Our self-respect was diminishing, our love, our kindness, our respect for ourselves and others diminished over time. But when we received salvation we became a new creation (a brand new building or asset) with a new value determined by God. There is no depreciation in God's economy; in fact, in God, there is only *appreciation*—meaning our value *increases*.

We must be careful because the devil will not stop trying to trip us up. Now we are in Christ, he will use various strategies to try to wear us out (Dan. 7:25) and if we are not careful as I mentioned earlier we will end up backsliding again without realizing it.

Come Out From Among Them

I sincerely believe that sometimes we have to separate from some friends, even *in church* in order to get to where God wants us to be. The people we associate with are sometimes the people who are hindering us spiritually. The Bible tells us of a man named Zacchaeus (Luke 19). Zacchaeus was rich because he was chief among the publicans[4]. Although he was a hated man because of his actions, he had a need. Zacchaeus had heard about Jesus and he had a desire to meet Him for himself. Zaccheus had a problem—the press[5]. The press followed Jesus everywhere he went and because Zacchaeus was vertically challenged (short) he would not be able to see Jesus. What could he do? What would *you* do? The same question applies to us today. Ask yourself, what do I do when I have a sincere desire to see Jesus but I cannot see Him because of the crowd I am in? The Bible tells us what Zacchaeus did and I believe we can learn a thing or two from him.

> *"And he ran before and climbed up into a sycamore tree to see him for he was to pass that way." (Luke 19:4)*

In order to see Jesus, Zacchaeus *ran ahead* of the crowd! If the group I am in is obstructing my vision of Jesus, I need to *get ahead* of the group. Zacchaeus knew that if he stayed in the crowd he was in he would not see Jesus for himself even though He was passing that way. Zacchaeus had never seen Jesus before so he probably did not know what He looked like. He had heard about the Man but what he had heard were other people's testimonies—he needed his own testimony.

Why Am I in The Crowd?

We need to understand that not everybody who came to see Jesus had the same motive. Some came to spy on him, some came to try and trap him. Some were there because they were with friends and family, while there were others who genuinely needed His help. All of these people were in the crowd. It is the same for us today, not everybody in the church desires a relationship with God. Some people come to church out of routine; some come to hear the choir sing or because they like the atmosphere, some are looking for a boyfriend/girlfriend or husband/wife, while there are others who have a genuine desire to meet with Jesus. The question is to which group do we belong? Zacchaeus' problem drove him to get ahead of the crowd. I truly believe that God will allow an obstacle to get in our way to compel us to make a decision. I am sure that some of Zacchaeus' friends were in the crowd, but they could not help him see Jesus. In order to see Jesus for himself, he had to separate himself from the crowd. I want you to notice that,

Jesus rarely deals with people in groups; he often deals with the individual.

Although Jesus was often followed by masses of people, we often read in the Gospels where He ministered to individuals while the crowd was there.
- The woman with the issue of blood (Luke 8:43–48)
- Blind Bartimaeus (Mk. 10:46–52)
- The centurion's servant (Luke 7:1–10)

In order for me to see Jesus, I need to separate myself from the crowd and reach him on my own. The next thing Zacchaeus did was climb up into a sycamore tree. Although he ran ahead, the crowd would eventually catch up with him, so he had to get *above* the crowd in order to see Jesus. He went to a higher level than those he was with. Sometimes just running ahead of the group I am in is not enough; sometimes I need to change *elevation* in order to catch a glimpse of Jesus. Praise may not be enough for me to see Jesus; I need to move from praise to *worship*. When Zaccheus changed elevation, he left the crowd at a lower level and got to a position where he could see Jesus for himself. When Zaccheus stood out from the crowd instead of blending in with them, he was able to get the attention of Jesus. Jesus ended up going to his house for dinner and Zaccheus' life was changed.

> *"And Zacchaeus stood, and said unto the Lord: Behold, Lord, the half of my goods I give to the poor; and if I have taken any thing from any man by false accusation, I restore him fourfold. And Jesus said unto him, This day is salvation come to this house, forasmuch as he also is a son of Abraham." (Luke 19:8–9)*

Let us stop trying to blend in with the crowd (the majority). It is ok to stand for something. If we stand for nothing, we will fall for anything. Dare to stand out. Do not be afraid to separate from the crowd so you can see Jesus for yourself. When He sees us He will bring salvation (deliverance) to our house.

Chapter 4

We Have a New Name

Conner, K (1992) says the following about names,

> *"The name always speaks of the nature, the character, the office or function of a person"* (p. 57). Merriam Webster (2014) defines a name as a word or phrase that constitutes the distinctive designation of a person or thing, a word or symbol used to designate an entity, a descriptive often disparaging epithet (p. 823).

Our Name Has Changed

We are not normal because our name has changed. When we look at a name, we can look at it as descriptive of a person's character, for example Nabal.

> *"Let not my lord, I pray thee, regard this man of Belial, even Nabal: for as his name is, so is he; Nabal is his name, and folly is with him: but I thine handmaid saw not the young men of my lord, whom thou didst send."* (1 Sam. 25:25)

We can also look at a name as being an epithet or label, for example prostitute, drug dealer and murderer are all names or labels we give to people. If we look at name changes in the Bible we see that oftentimes the change of name occurred at a critical moment in the individual's life. To illustrate this, we will look at two Bible characters who had their names changed.

Jacob

The name Jacob means heel-grabber, trickster, or supplanter. He was called Jacob because although his twin brother Esau came out of the womb first, when Jacob came out he grabbed hold of Esau's heel. As they grew older Esau became a skilled hunter while Jacob was content to dwell indoors (Gen. 25:27). Isaac loved Esau but his wife Rebekah loved Jacob. One day Esau came home from hunting and saw that Jacob had made pottage[6]. It appears that Esau had had a long day in the field because the Bible says he was faint (Gen. 25:29). When he asked Jacob for some of the pottage he had prepared, Jacob made him a strange offer.

"Sell me this day thy birthright." (Gen. 25:31)

Esau did not hesitate to accept the offer rationalizing that the birthright would be of no use to him if he died of starvation It seems however that Jacob was more aware of the significance of the birthright because he made Esau swear to sell it to him. It is important to understand something at this point; Esau was **not** tricked into selling his birthright, nobody put a gun to his head or a knife to his throat. He was not coerced or blackmailed, he made a conscious decision to sell his birthright because he placed little value on it. The Bible puts it this way,

"Esau despised his birthright." (Gen. 25:34)

Many years later when Isaac was old and his eyesight was all but gone, he called Esau and asked him to go hunting for venison and prepare a meal for him, after which he would pronounce a blessing upon him. After overhearing the conversation Rebekah convinced Jacob to disguise himself as his brother in order to receive the blessing. Although Isaac was suspicious at first he eventually believed that Esau had brought him the venison and he proceeded to bless (who he thought was) his firstborn. When Esau returned from hunting and preparing his meal, Isaac realized he had blessed Jacob instead of Esau. Esau blamed his brother saying,

> *"Is not he rightly named Jacob? For he hath supplanted me these two times: he took away my birthright; and, behold, now he hath taken away my blessing." (Gen. 27:36)*

While it is fair to say that Jacob stole the blessing, it was Esau who sold his birthright. Esau was not thinking rationally so he determined to kill Jacob when their father died. Rebekah discovered Esau' intentions and sent Jacob away to her brother Laban (Gen. 27:43). Jacob was away from home for at least twenty years[7]. After 20 years Jacob left Laban's house and sent his servants with gifts to Esau in an attempt to appease his anger. They returned explaining that Esau was coming to meet him with 400 servants. This news filled Jacob with so much fear that he divided his household into two groups and sent them ahead of him across the river. He thought if Esau attacked the first group then at least the second group would escape. Jacob sent the two groups across the ford Jabbok at night and was left alone. It is at this point that Jacob wrestled with a man[8] until daybreak. We are not told why they were wrestling; maybe Jacob thought the man was Esau. It soon became apparent however that this was no ordinary man. The man could not prevail over Jacob (such was Jacob's tenacity) so he touched the hallow of his thigh so that it became out of joint. Jacob still would not let go of the man so the man asked Jacob his name. After Jacob acknowledged who he was, his name was changed from Jacob (trickster) to Israel (contender with God). It was then that Jacob realised he had been in an encounter with God.

Jacob was no longer a supplanter; he was now a prince. He was a different person when he met Esau the second time. In the same way when we have had an encounter with God there must be a change in our lives. People may have known who we were before our encounter with God but remember,

"We have a new name!"

Saul

Saul of Tarsus was a Pharisee who persecuted the early church. Saul possessed dual nationality because, although he was a Jew by birth (Phil. 3:5), he inherited Roman citizenship from his father (Acts 22:25–28). As a Pharisee, it would have been normal for him to go by his Jewish name, Saul. When he later brought the Gospel message to the Gentiles, he is referred to by his Roman name[9] (Acts 13:9).

When Stephen[10] became the first martyr, Saul consented to his death; he was responsible for watching over the coats of those throwing the stones at Stephen (Acts 7:58; 22:20). Saul obtained authority from the chief priests to travel to Damascus to arrest those who belonged to the way[11]. On his way to arrest the disciples, Saul was placed under arrest himself by the Lord (Acts 9:3–8). He was blind for three days until a disciple called Ananias prayed and laid hands on him for his sight to be restored (Acts 9:9–18). After spending some time with the disciples in Damascus he immediately began to preach Christ in the synagogues (Acts 9:19–20). Every one that heard him preach could not believe that this was the same Saul who had been persecuting those who called on the name of Jesus

> "But all that heard him were amazed, and said; Is not he that destroyed them which called on this name in Jerusalem, and came hither for that intent, that he might bring them bound unto the chief priests" (Acts 9:21).

Even the disciples in Jerusalem were suspicious when Saul tried to join them.

> *"And when Saul was come to Jerusalem, he assayed to join himself to the disciples: but they were afraid of him, and believed not that he was a disciple." (Acts 9:26)*

It was not until Barnabas brought him to the apostles and shared Saul's testimony and his own experience of the new Saul that the disciples accepted him (Acts 9:26–28). There is an important lesson to be learned here. Sometimes people will not believe that we have changed. Before Saul met the Lord on the road to Damascus his name was *"persecutor"* but after his encounter with Jesus Christ his name became *"preacher."* Saul was judged based on who he was *before* his Damascus Road experience not who he was *after*. In the same way, it does not matter who we were *before* we came to Christ; what matters is who we are *after* our encounter with Him. We may have had a name before we met Jesus, maybe it was *"murderer," "pedophile," "drunkard," "prostitute,"* or *"drug dealer."* But when we met Jesus Christ something happened. Sometimes even our own family or brethren do not believe we have changed from who we were before and they may still call us by our old name. We do not need to defend or justify who we are now—we just need to let our lifestyle testify that,

"We have a new name!

Chapter 5
Presentation Is Important

"I beseech you therefore, brethren, by the mercies of God, that ye present your bodies a living sacrifice, holy, acceptable unto God, which is your reasonable service." (Rom. 12:1)

There are some Christians who appear to live their lives as though presentation before God is not important. *"Render your heart not your garments"* was a phrase I heard from Christians many times when I was growing up and I still hear it even today. When the Bible says, "rend your heart and not your garments" it is referring to the condition of our hearts not our clothing. The phrase "render your heart" does not appear in the Bible. The Scripture *actually* says,

*"Therefore also now, saith the L*ORD*, turn ye even to me with all your heart, and with fasting, and with weeping, and with mourning: And rend your heart, and not your garments, and turn unto the L*ORD *your God: for he is gracious and merciful, slow to anger, and of great kindness, and repenteth him of the evil." (Joel 2:12–13)*

The rending (or tearing) of a garment was an outward sign of sorrow (see Genesis 37:34; 2 Samuel 1:11; Joshua 7:6; 2 Samuel 13:19 for examples). The problem was the people were only displaying an outward sign of repentance rather than exhibiting true repentance from the heart (see Psalms 51:17).

Allow me to show that as a child of God, our presentation is important. In the above scripture the Apostle Paul exhorted the saints in Rome to present their bodies to God as a living sacrifice. What did he mean by this request and what did it entail? Under the Old Testament sacrificial system, there were specific instructions that had to be adhered to when bringing an offering to the Lord. The first seven chapters of the book of Leviticus deal with the five principal offerings (burnt, grain, peace, sin, and trespass offering) given to Moses and the instances in which they were to be offered. When we read these chapters we notice that the common criteria for the animal that was to be sacrificed was that it had to be without blemish. Here are some examples:

> "If his offering be a burnt sacrifice of the herd, let him offer a male **without blemish**: he shall offer it of his own voluntary will at the door of the tabernacle of the congregation before the LORD." (Lev. 1:3)

> "And if his oblation be a sacrifice of peace offering, if he offer it of the herd; whether it be a male or female, he shall offer it **without blemish** before the LORD" (Lev. 3:1)

> "If the priest that is anointed do sin according to the sin of the people; then let him bring for his sin, which he hath sinned, a young bullock **without blemish** unto the LORD for a sin offering." (Lev. 4:3)

> "If a soul commit a trespass, and sin through ignorance, in the holy things of the LORD; then he shall bring for his trespass unto the LORD a ram **without blemish** out of the flocks, with thy estimation by shekels of silver, after the shekel of the sanctuary, for a trespass offering:" (Lev. 5:15)

Of the five offerings prescribed to Moses, only the grain offering (Lev. 2) allowed anything other than an animal to be sacrificed[12]. Notice the stipulation "*without blemish*" is used when referring to the animal to be sacrificed. But what does this mean? The phrase '*without blemish*' comes from the Hebrew word *tamim*. According to the Hebrew-Greek Key Word Study Bible (2011) or Strong's (Number 8549) *Tamim* means *entire* (literally, figuratively, or morally) *whole, complete, perfect, sound* (free from blemishes in sacrificial victims), *faultless* (p.1675). The animal was not permitted to have any physical defects, marks, and so forth. The same principle applied to the priests that were to minister in the Tabernacle.

> "Then the LORD spoke to Moses, saying, [17] "Say to Aaron, 'Throughout their generations none of your descendants who has any [physical] defect shall approach [the altar] to present the food of his God. For no man who has a defect shall approach [God's altar as a priest]: no man who is blind or lame, or who has a disfigured face, or any deformed limb, or a man who has a broken foot or a broken hand, [20] or a hunchback or a dwarf, or one who has a defect in his eye or eczema or scabs or crushed testicles. [21] No man among the descendants of Aaron the priest who has a [physical] defect and is disfigured or deformed is to approach [the altar] to present the offerings of the LORD by fire. He has a defect; he shall not approach [the altar] to present the food of his God." (Lev. 21:16–21 AMP)

God wants us to be without blemish; without the blemish of hatred, malice, unforgiveness, lust, or anger. God wants us to be whole, not broken, not twisted or corrupt, not filthy, or stained but *whole*.

It Must Be A 'Living Dead' Sacrifice

The Apostle encourages us to present our bodies as a *living* sacrifice (no more dead sacrifices). The animals sacrificed in the Old Testament were killed and offered in a prescribed way, but we are called to be a *'living dead'* sacrifice. What do I mean by *'living dead?'* I mean that our flesh must die in order for the Spirit of God to reign in our lives. Paul told the Corinthian church that he died on a daily basis (1 Cor. 15:31) so *everyday*, we have to mortify (kill) our flesh (its urges, desires, and feelings) and offer it up in sacrifice to God. In his book *Godchasers*, Tommy Tenny (1998) uses the phrase "*Dead man walking*" to refer to a prisoner on death row who was walking to the place of his execution (p. 72). When we crucify our flesh on a daily basis, then we can truly be dead men and women walking.

It Must Be Holy

Paul then states the living sacrifice should be "holy, acceptable unto God." Note that Paul says *'holy, acceptable unto God'* not *'holy and acceptable.'* Why? Because if we are holy then God will accept us, for the Bible says that without holiness no man shall see the Lord (Heb. 12:14).

What is holiness? Many today equate holiness to the size of a hat, the length of a skirt, or simply being makeup free. These are merely outward measurements of holiness that primarily apply to women. If you notice not much is said regarding what constitutes 'holiness' for men so this cannot be all holiness consists of. Holiness is more than maintaining an outward standard; it is the very essence and character of God within the believer. The Lord said to the children of Israel,

"Be ye holy for I am holy." (Lev. 20:7)

It is possible to maintain an outward standard and still not be holy; many people wear the 'right clothes' yet they are negative, judgmental, critical, proud, covetous, envious, and rebellious. The Pharisees 'looked holy' but they were hypocrites; they felt they were better than everybody else (Luke 18:10–12). I believe the Pharisee 'spirit' still exists today. People with the Pharisee spirit still come to church but the church is not in them. Pharisees are those who know what the Word says but do not live by what the Word says. Pharisees cannot handle the move of God so they are uncomfortable when the Holy Spirit is moving in church. Pharisees prefer 'business as usual' and try to lock the move of the Holy Spirit in their 'order of service' shaped-box. God wants the heart of His people to be right first before the outward appearance. When the Holy Spirit is Lord of our heart, we will have no problem surrendering what we wear to Him. Many today wear what they want because they refuse to yield this area of their life totally to the Lord. The late Bishop Norman L. Wagner put it this way

"If He is not Lord of ALL, He is not Lord AT ALL!"

It Is Who Are, Not What We Wear
I remember someone once put it like this "inward holiness produces outward righteousness" and I cannot argue with this statement. Holiness should come from our spirit and emanate through what we wear and how we relate to people. It should be our attitude, not just when we are in church but when we are at work, school, shopping for groceries or putting petrol (gas) in our cars. It is important also to note that holiness does not mean *ugliness*. Some Christians seem to think that because they are holy they cannot smile or laugh. It is as though they must have a grave look on their faces at all times, like they were baptized in a pool of salt water and lemon juice.

Our Reasonable Service
Paul said something profound concerning our presentation before God. After we have done all we can do to present

ourselves holy before Almighty God; after we have fasted and prayed and mortified the deeds of this sinful flesh; after we have forgiven and asked for forgiveness; after we have submitted to His will, then we can *start* to serve God. He concluded that this is our *reasonable* service, which seems to suggest that this is the *bare* minimum, the *very least* we can do. After all that Jesus has done for us, the *least* we can do is present ourselves holy before Him, yet for many of us, myself included at times, the living holy part seems to be the most challenging, even more so if I have not surrendered totally to God's will (which is what the burnt offering symbolized).

Gift-Wrapped Presents

Allow me to give you an illustration. In the natural, when we buy a present for someone we love we generally make sure that the present is worthy of the person to whom we are giving it. These days many of us gift-wrap our presents and we take extra care to ensure there are no creases in the wrapping paper and that everything looks good. The wrapping paper we purchase sometimes gives an indication of the value of gift inside as nobody when buying a gift spends more on the wrapping than the actual gift. If someone gives you a gift, wrapped in glittering gold paper you would expect the gift to be something special. So it is with our outward appearance (how we adorn ourselves), this should be the wrapping paper of what is on the inside of us—a godly character). God wants our outward appearance to be a reflection of Christ just as Jesus' character showed that the Father dwelt within him.

Cain and Abel—Contrasting Presents

Cain and Abel both presented offerings to the Lord (Gen. 4).

> *"And in the course of time Cain brought to the L*ORD *an offering of the fruit of the ground. ⁴ But Abel brought [an offering of] the [finest] firstborn of his flock and the fat portions." (Gen. 4:3–4 AMP)*

Cain's offering was from the fruit of the ground because he was a tiller of the ground (a farmer), while Abel's offering was from his flock (he was a shepherd). The Bible says,

> *"And the LORD had respect unto Abel and to his offering: But unto Cain and to his offering he had not respect." (Gen. 4:4b-5)*

There are differing schools of thought regarding the reason why Cain's offering was rejected and Abel's accepted. Some say that Abel's offering was accepted because he offered a lamb. They say he was in line with God redemptive plan (Jesus being the lamb slain before the foundation of the world and blood being the subsequent method of atonement under the Mosaic law). While I agree with this school of thought, allow me to look at it from a different perspective. God had respect unto Abel **and** unto his offering. We noted earlier that under the Mosaic Law, the law of the grain offering did not require an animal to be killed so you could argue that if the grain offering would later become acceptable then why was Cain's offering rejected if his offering came from the ground? In addition, under Mosaic Law, if a person could not afford an animal he or she could offer flour for a sin offering (see Leviticus 5:11–13). So why was Cain rejected? What I saw was the fact that Cain's offering was from the *fruit of the ground* while Abel (according to the Amplified Bible) offered the finest firstborn from his flock and the fat. In addition, the Bible says that God had respect unto *Abel* **and** to his offering, which means that God did not just look at *what* was offered, but He also looked at the *offerer* of the offering. God looked at the motive (the heart) behind Abel's offering and accepted both him and his offering. The writer of the book of Hebrews states,

> *"By faith Abel offered unto God a more excellent sacrifice than Cain, by which he obtained witness that he was righteous, God testifying of*

his gifts: and by it he being dead yet speaketh."
(Heb. 11:4)

I believe that Abel's offering was driven by faith, while Cain's was not; which is why both Abel and his offering were accepted. I believe it was faith that moved Abel to give God the best of his flock while Cain just offered from what was available; his offering was not driven by faith. Paul states to the Roman brethren that *"whatsoever is not of faith is sin."* (Rom. 14:23) Cain was upset with God and had to be cautioned about his attitude (Gen. 4:7). If Cain's attitude was right he would have repented and brought an acceptable offering to the Lord but instead of heeding God's warning he killed his brother in cold blood (Gen. 4:8). We too can have the same attitude if we are not careful. When God is blessing our brother do we throw a temper tantrum? Do we get upset? Do we criticize him or try to kill him (assassinate his character)? Do we get upset with God for accepting his sacrifice of worship while rejecting ours? Do we covet our brother's blessing or do we go directly to the giver of the blessing and say, "Lord, I repent!" It is the *offerer* God wants first *then* the offering. Our heart must be right when we present ourselves before God. When our heart is right we will not only present an acceptable sacrifice to the Lord, but we will **be** an acceptable sacrifice.

Chapter 6

What Do You See?

What is Sight?

Merriam Webster Collegiate Dictionary (2014) defines sight as the process, power or function of seeing; specifically: the physical sense by which light stimuli received by the eye are interpreted by the brain and constructed into a representation of the position, shape, brightness and usu. color of objects in space (p. 1158). When you look at the situation you are in, what do you see? I want to show that not only is what we see important but what we *believe* about what we see is just as, if not more, important than what we see.

Two Spies Saw Victory while Ten saw Defeat

In Numbers 13 the Lord commanded Moses to send men to search out the land of Canaan.

> *"Send thou men, that they may search the land of Canaan, which I give unto the children of Israel: of every tribe of their fathers shall ye send a man, every one a ruler among them." (Num. 13:2)*

Moses chose 12 men who were the heads of the children of Israel and gave them specific instructions. They were to report on the condition of the land and the people.

> "And Moses sent them to spy out the land of Canaan, and said unto them, Get you up this way southward, and go up into the mountain: And see the land, what it is, and the people that dwelleth therein, whether they be strong or weak, few or many; And what the land is that they dwell in, whether it be good or bad; and what cities they be that they dwell in, whether in tents, or in strong holds: And what the land is, whether it be fat or lean, whether there be wood therein, or not. And be ye of good courage, and bring of the fruit of the land. Now the time was the time of the first ripe grapes." (Num. 13:18–20)

After 40 days of reconnaissance, the spies returned and presented their findings to Moses, Aaron, and the rest of the congregation. This was their report.

> "We came unto the land whither thou sentest us, and surely it floweth with milk and honey; and this is the fruit of it. Nevertheless the people be strong that dwell in the land, and the cities are walled, and very great: and moreover we saw the children of Anak. The Amalekites dwell in the land of the south: and the Hittites, and the Jebusites, and the Amorites, dwell in the mountains: and the Canaanites dwell by the sea, and by the coast of Jordan." (Num. 13:27–29)

At this point Caleb tried to settle the commotion, as he must have sensed there was some concern about what had just been said.

> *"And Caleb stilled the people before Moses, and said, "Let us go up at once, and possess it; for we are well able to overcome it." (Num. 13:30)*

Caleb's response to the report was basically, "We can do this!" Caleb was one of the 12 spies that were sent so he saw exactly what the other spies saw, but his response was

> *"We can overcome these people, what are we waiting for?"*

Unfortunately, the men that went up with him said,

> *"We be not able to go up against the people; for they are stronger than we." (verse.31)*

They then delivered the following report.

> *"The land through which we went, in spying it out, is a land that devours its inhabitants. And all the people that we saw in it are men of great stature. There we saw the Nephilim (the sons of Anak are part of the Nephilim); and we were like grasshoppers in our own sight, and so we were in their sight." (Num. 13:32–33 AMP)*

The other spies were basically saying that Israel should not go up because the enemy was stronger than them and they would lose. The land, which they previously testified as being fruitful, was now a land that would consume the entire congregation. In addition, they saw giants in the land, and not just any giants but the sons of Anak who were descendants of the giants. They declared that they felt like grasshoppers compared to the giants and that the giants probably saw them as grasshoppers as well.

I'm sure if it happened today, Caleb would have said,

"You should have gone to Specsavers!"

The Bible calls the report they gave an evil one (Num. 13:32), but why was the report evil? I believe the report was evil because it was a report of unbelief and fear rather than a report of faith and confidence. The Bible says that,

"whatsoever is not of faith is sin." (Rom. 14:23)

Fear is sometimes used as an acronym meaning *F*alse *E*vidence *A*ppearing *R*eal. How did the 10 spies know how they appeared to the sons of Anak? The answer is they had absolutely no idea, fear made them see something that was not there.

Faith vs. Fear

The Bible says that faith comes by hearing the Word of God (Rom. 10:17). I believe that fear also comes by hearing, hearing the word of men. How often have we listened to the word of men and have believed their report over the Word of God? We go into the doctor's office and he tells us that we have a life threatening illness and we only have 6 months to live. Instead of requesting a second opinion from the *Great* Physician we accept the word of man as the final authority on our situation. I remember seeing the following picture on Facebook and I immediately saved the image to my phone, I think it perfectly shows the two responses we can have to fear.

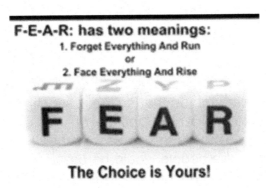

I believe fear is a virus that is transmitted orally and received audibly. In this case the fear was so contagious that when the congregation heard the evil report they all cried to the Lord and began to murmur against Moses and Aaron. Imagine listening to the sound of over two million men, women, and children crying out to the Lord in fear? After being delivered from hundreds of years of slavery in Egypt, they now wanted to go back to Egypt or die in the wilderness? Jehovah had brought them through the Rea Sea and had provided them with food (manna, quails) and water. Now just when they were on the verge of walking into the promises of God, they encountered an obstacle that challenged their faith—and they wanted to turn back.

> *"So they said one to another, "Let us appoint a [new] leader and return to Egypt." (Num. 14:4 AMP)*

Joshua and Caleb were so upset that they tore their clothes in distress. Listen to what they said to the people,

> *The land, which we passed through to search it, is an exceeding good land. If the LORD delight in us, then he will bring us into this land, and give it us; a land which floweth with milk and honey. Only rebel not ye against the LORD, neither fear ye the people of the land; for they are bread for us: their defence is departed from them, and the LORD is with us: fear them not." (Num. 14:7–9)*

I believe Moses told all the spies that the land had already been given to them by the Lord (see Numbers 13:2). Joshua and Caleb *saw,* not just a good land, but an **exceeding** good land. They understood that if God was with them, then they would be able to enter the land that He had given them. There was no need to fear the people because the Lord was with them. In fact, the people would be *bread* for them. The word bread is the Hebrew word *lechem, which* means bread, food, or grain. We eat food in order to gain physical strength so these people would be the means by which the children of Israel would strengthen their faith. Finally, they saw that the people were defenseless. This was in stark contrast to what the other spies said (see Num. 13:32–33).

All twelve sp*ies* saw the land and the people but only *two believed* what they saw. Ten men managed to convince over two million Israelites that what they *saw* could not be overcome. Because Israel believed the evil report, the Lord allowed them to wander for 40 years until everyone except Caleb and Joshua died in the wilderness.

Rehab's Testimony

I want you to look at the testimony of Rahab when Joshua sent spies to look at Jericho (Josh. 2:9–11). Compare the testimony of Rahab below with the report of the ten spies (Num. 13:27– 29) and then read the report of Caleb and Joshua (Num. 14:7–9).

> *"And she said unto the men, I know that the Lord hath given you the land, and that your terror is fallen upon us, and that all the inhabitants of the land faint because of you. For we have heard how the Lord dried up the water of the Red sea for you, when ye came out of Egypt; and what ye did unto the two kings of the Amorites, that were on the other side Jordan, Sihon and Og, whom ye utterly destroyed. And as soon as we had heard these things, our hearts did melt, neither did there remain any more courage in any man, because of you: for the Lord your God, he is God in heaven above, and in earth beneath." (Josh. 2:9–11)*

The Spies' Evil Report

> *But the men that went up with him said, We be not able to go up against the people; for they are stronger than we. And they brought up an evil*

report of the land which they had searched unto the children of Israel, saying, The land, through which we have gone to search it, is a land that eateth up the inhabitants thereof; and all the people that we saw in it are men of a great stature. And there we saw the giants, the sons of Anak, which come of the giants: and we were in our own sight as grasshoppers, and so we were in their sight." (Num. 13:31–33)

As we can see the testimony of Caleb and Joshua was based on what they saw and *believed* was true. The testimony of Rahab years later proves that what the ten spies saw and reported was borne out of fear (False Evidence Appearing Real). We cannot afford to be like the ten spies, we serve a God who is greater than any opposition we will ever encounter and He is able to deliver us in any situation.

An Inside Job

In 2 Kings 6, we read about a war between Syria and Israel. Whenever the king of Syria decided the location for his camp, the Lord would reveal the location of the camp to the prophet Elisha. Elisha would then inform the king of Israel who would avoid that particular location. This happened on multiple occasions, which prompted the king of Syria to conclude there was a double agent in his ranks. After questioning his officials, it was explained to him that Israel had an unfair advantage. Israel had a prophet (Elisha) who was revealing the location of his camp.

What You See Does Not Always Make Sense

The king of Syria sent spies to locate Elisha and dispatched his entire army to ensure his capture. Thousands of soldiers, chariots and horses surrounded the city of Dothan at night (2 Kings 6:14). When Elisha's servant rose early the next morning and looked outside, he saw the predicament they were in, he immediately said to Elisha,

What Do You See?

> *"Alas, my master! how shall we do?" (2 Kgs 6:15)*

Elisha's response seems puzzling at first,

> *"Fear not: for they that be with us are more than they that be with them." (2 Kgs 6:16)*

What are you talking about Elisha? What do you mean we have more on our side? Surely you can see the numbers that are against us? Notice Elisha tells his servant not to be *fearful*. What the servant **saw** made him afraid. He could not think of a way of escape or a way of overcoming the numbers so he was basically asking his master "how are we going to get out of this one?" It would seem that Elisha's exhortation not to be fearful was not enough because Elisha prayed,

> *"LORD, I pray thee, open his eyes, that he may see." (2 Kgs 6:17)*

Wait a minute, why would Elisha make this request? Surely the eyes of the servant were open already? Although his eyes were open, he could not **see** what Elisha saw so his spiritual *eyes* needed to be opened. When the Lord opened the servant's eyes, he saw that not only did the enemy surround them, but horses and chariots of fire *surrounded* the enemy as well! Elisha's servant saw one thing but Elisha saw and believed something else. What the servant saw filled him with fear, what Elisha saw and believed filled him with confidence. So, I will ask the question again, when you look at your situation, what do you see? If what you see fills your heart with fear, then ask the Lord to open your eyes so you can see clearly. Remember the Word says,

> *"We walk by faith, not by sight." (2 Cor. 5:7)*

Chapter 7

We Will Not Bow

> *"Be it known unto thee, O King, that we will not serve thy gods, nor worship the golden image which thou hast set up." (Dan. 3:18)*

The biblical story of the three Hebrew boys is set in the period while Judah was in Babylonian captivity. I have heard many people (young and old) exhort and preach about Shadrach, Meshach and Abednego being thrown into the fiery furnace. In Daniel 1 King Nebuchadnezzar laid siege to, and captured, the city of Jerusalem during the reign of Jehoiakin (King of Judah). Nebuchadnezzar commissioned the master of his eunuchs to go through the tribe of Judah and select from them the best among the children of Israel, the king's seed, and the princes. They were to be,

> *"Children in whom was no blemish, but well favoured, and skilful in all wisdom, and cunning in knowledge, and understanding science, and such as had ability in them to stand in the king's palace, and whom they might teach the learning and the tongue of the Chaldeans. (Dan. 1:4)*

Nebuchadnezzar knew that by taking the best people from the nation he had just conquered, that nation would be unable to recover. The Babylonians endeavored to assimilate their captives into Chaldean culture by changing their language, their speech, and their diet. Nebuchadnezzar wanted to erase every trace of their identity so, as well as changing their language, he also changed their names. When I was growing up, whenever I heard anyone speak about the three Hebrew boys, it was always Shadrach, Meshach and Abednego. But many people often forget that those were not their original names. According to Daniel 1:6 their Hebrew names were Hananiah, Mishael and Azariah. The name Hananiah means "Yahweh is gracious," Mishael means, "Who is like Yahweh," and Azariah means, "Yahweh has helped." The prince of the eunuchs gave them Chaldean (or Babylonian) names. Shadrach means the command of Aku (a Babylonian moon god), Meshach supposedly means the servant of a Chaldean god, and Abednego means the servant of Nabu/Nego (another Babylonian god).

The Enemy Wants to Change Your Name

Children of God the enemy wants to change our identity. The enemy wants to give us a worldly name; he wants to change the way we think, the way we speak, and the way we live. Babylon represents the world so it is clear that the enemy wants us to think like, speak like, and live like the world. The question is, to which name are we answering? Hananiah, Mishael, and Azariah were names that glorified Jehovah and reminded the Hebrew boys who they were, but the eunuch gave them names that glorified the gods of Babylon. They fed all the captives with the King's meat and the wine that he drank. In other words, they tried to fully integrate them into the Babylonian system. But Daniel purposed in his heart that he would not defile himself with the king's meat (Daniel 1:8). He knew the meat would have been sacrificed to idols and he wanted to remain pure before his God. There is a saying "when in Rome, do as the Romans do," but Daniel did not ascribe to this philosophy; he was determined to maintain his identity and purity regardless of the consequences. The Lord had already given Daniel favor in the eyes of the princes of the eunuchs (Dan. 1:9) so Daniel was able to persuade the eunuch to let him abstain from eating the king's meat. He asked if he and his companions could be given pulses (vegetables, fruits, and grains) to eat and water to drink for ten days. After ten days, the countenances of Daniel and his companions were far healthier than those who ate the King's meat (Daniel 1:5).

Nebuchadnezzar's Golden Image

In Daniel 2, Nebuchadnezzar had a troubling dream that none of his council of magicians and astrologers could interpret. After Daniel told the king what he had dreamed and gave him the interpretation, both he and his companions were promoted to positions of prominence within Babylon. Daniel 3 begins with Nebuchadnezzar commissioning the construction of a golden image, which was positioned in the plain of Dura, in the province of Babylon. The height of the image was threescore (sixty) cubits and the breadth (or width) of the image was six cubits. In today's measurements this equates to a height of ninety feet and a width of nine feet at a size ratio of 10:1. I tried to get a picture in my mind's eye of how tall this image would have been. I tried to see if it was comparable to any statues or monuments in the United Kingdom to get a better appreciation of its size. The closest I could find was the Albert Memorial (180 feet from toe to tip) and Nelson's column (170 feet) both of which are located in London, England. Nebuchadnezzar's image would have been approximately half the height of the Albert Memorial or just over half the height of Nelson's column.

The Albert Memorial

Nelson's Column

While I was researching the size of the image there was something else that I came across. The image that Nebuchadnezzar commissioned was the same dimensions as an obelisk[13]. It is said that both the Egyptian and Babylonian ancient occult religions included sexual immorality in their satanic ceremonies and that the obelisk is shaped to look like a male phallus. Another example of an obelisk is the Washington Monument, which has the exact size ratio (10:1) as Nebuchadnezzar's image. Below is picture of the Washington Monument, as well as an artist's impression of what the image may have looked like.

Washington's Monument

Nebuchadnezzar's Image

Nebuchadnezzar had it proclaimed that at the sound of the various instruments of music (cornet, flute, harp, sackbut, dulcimer, etc.) everyone in the kingdom should fall down and worship the golden image that he had commissioned (Dan. 2:14–15). Whoever did not worship the image would be thrown into the midst of a burning fiery furnace. Nebuchadnezzar had set Hananiah, Mishael, and Azariah over affairs of the province of Babylon at the request of Daniel (Dan. 2:49) so the edict applied to them as well as the rest of the inhabitants of Babylon. When the time came that the sound of the music was heard, all the people of Babylon (except for these three young men) fell down and worshipped the image (Dan. 3:7). The Chaldeans brought this to the attention of King Nebuchadnezzar.

> *"There are certain Jews whom thou hast set over the affairs of the province of Babylon, Shadrach, Meshach, and Abednego; these men, O king, have not regarded thee: they serve not thy gods, nor worship the golden image which thou hast set up."* (Dan. 3:12)

It is clear that the Chaldeans had a problem with Hananiah, Mishael, and Azariah because they were now in a position of authority. They reminded Nebuchadnezzar that he was the one who put them in authority and now they were rebelling against his orders! They knew how to push his buttons. They knew if they mentioned him, his gods and his beloved image that it would be enough to get their desired response. As soon as Nebuchadnezzar heard the accusations, he immediately summoned Shadrach, Meshach, and Abednego to be brought before him (verse 13). Firstly, he enquired whether the allegations were true.

> *"Is it true, O Shadrach, Meshach, and Abednego, do not ye serve my gods, nor worship the golden image which I have set up?"* (Dan. 3:14)

He then gave them a further opportunity to comply with his edict.

> *"Now if ye be ready that at what time ye hear the sound of the cornet, flute, harp, sackbut, psaltery, and dulcimer, and all kinds of musick, ye fall down and worship the image which I have made; well: but if ye worship not, ye shall be cast the same hour into the midst of a burning fiery furnace; and who is that God that shall deliver you out of my hands?"* (Dan. 3:15)

This is how Shadrach, Meshach, and Abednego responded to the king,

> *"O Nebuchadnezzar, it is not necessary for us to answer you on this point. If our God whom we serve is able to deliver us from the burning fiery furnace, He will deliver us out of your hand, O king. But if not, let it be known to you, O king, that we will not serve your gods or worship the golden image which you have set up!" (Dan. 3:16–18 AMP)*

The three Hebrew boys did not even address the allegations made against them by the Chaldeans because it was not necessary. They stated defiantly and categorically that they would not worship, in other words

"We will not bow."

Whether or not our God is able to deliver us from the furnace, our response is the same,

"We will not bow!"

They were willing to be burned but they were not willing to worship another god. The response of the three young men infuriated King Nebuchadnezzar so much that he requested the furnace to be heated seven times hotter than normal (Dan. 3:19). He then commanded the strongest men in his army to bind up Shadrach, Meshach, and Abednego and throw them into the fiery furnace.

> *"Therefore because the king's commandment was urgent and the furnace exceedingly hot, the flame and sparks from the fire killed those men who handled Shadrach, Meshach, and Abednego." (Dan. 3.22 AMP)*

These three young men were thrown *bound* into the furnace (verse. 23) but when Nebuchadnezzar looked into the furnace (presumably from a distance) he saw something strange,

> "Did not we cast three men bound into the midst of the fire? They answered and said unto the king, True, O king. He answered and said, Lo, I see four men loose, walking in the midst of the fire, and they have no hurt; and the form of the fourth is like the Son of God." (Dan. 3: 24–25)

Nebuchadnezzar had previously asked to know the God that would be able to deliver the three Hebrew boys out of his hands (Dan. 3:15) but he probably did not expect to see Him so quickly! I want you to notice three things:
1. Three men were thrown bound into the fire but four men were seen walking around loose in the midst of the fire!
2. They were *in* the fire but they had *no hurt!*
3. The fourth man was only seen after they were *in the fire!*

There are many things we could say about this verse but one thing we can all be sure of: God is *always* on time. He promised that we would not go through trouble on our own but He would be with us.

> "When thou passest through the waters, **I will be with thee**; and through the rivers, they shall not overflow thee: when thou walkest through the fire, thou shalt not be burned; neither shall the flame kindle upon thee." (Isa. 43:2)

Are We Bowing Down to The Image?

> "Nebuchadnezzar the king made an image of gold, whose height was threescore cubits, and the breadth thereof six cubits: he set it up in the plain of Dura, in the province of Babylon." (Dan. 3:1)

According to the Hebrew-Greek Key Word Study Bible (1991), the Hebrew word translated as image in this verse is *tselem,* which means image, likeness, resemblance, illusion; a representative figure, an idol; a phantom, nothingness (p.1675). Merriam Webster's Dictionary (2014) defines the word image as
1.—A reproduction or imitation of the form of a person or thing.
2.—A visual representation of something (p. 619).

If we are looking for ninety-foot tall golden statue in Iraq (modern day Babylon), we will not find one. The enemy of our souls is much more subtle than that. I believe that the image the enemy uses today is people. By using people, satan (the god of this world) has set up his idolatrous representation in the media (television, magazines, online) in order to influence the world to bow down to him.. We have established that King Nebuchadnezzar's image was an obelisk and how that sexual immorality played an important in occult rituals and practices. including secret societies. You may be surprised to know the number (and names) of celebrities, pop stars, musicians, and even Hollywood actors and actresses who are part of secret societies that participate in these satanic rituals. They use esoteric and or occult symbols, secret messages and signs to show who they worship (e.g. clothes, hand-signs or gestures they make when they pose for pictures in public or when they are performing). To most of us these signs appear to be innocent enough but many have a hidden meaning that most of us know nothing about. Many artists in the music industry (hip-hop, pop, R&B, heavy metal, rock and roll, etc.) are actually satanists. They have sold their souls to obtain wealth and fame in exchange for influencing people through their music. The enemy knows a thing or two about music and how influential it is considering his former position.

> *"How art thou fallen from heaven, O Lucifer, son of the morning! how art thou cut down to the ground, which didst weaken the nations! For thou hast said in thine heart, I will ascend into*

> heaven, I will exalt my throne above the stars of God: I will sit also upon the mount of the congregation, in the sides of the north: I will ascend above the heights of the clouds; I will be like the most High. Yet thou shalt be brought down to hell, to the sides of the pit." (Isa. 14:12–15)

> "Thou hast been in Eden the garden of God; every precious stone was thy covering, the sardius, topaz, and the diamond, the beryl, the onyx, and the jasper, the sapphire, the emerald, and the carbuncle, and gold: the workmanship of thy tabrets and of thy pipes was prepared in thee in the day that thou wast created. Thou art the anointed cherub that covereth; and I have set thee so: thou wast upon the holy mountain of God; thou hast walked up and down in the midst of the stones of fire. Thou wast perfect in thy ways from the day that thou wast created, till iniquity was found in thee." (Ezek. 28:13–15)

Let us take the music industry as an example. The term back masking refers to the recording technique whereby a sound or message is (deliberately) recorded backward onto a track that is supposed to be played forward. Back masked words are unintelligible noise when played forward, but when played backwards are clear speech. Many people (particularly young people) today feel that there is nothing wrong with listening and dancing to their favourite secular artist not realising that the music may contain a completely different message to the one to which they are listening. How many young people go to these concerts, buy the memorabilia, and even change their vocabulary and appearance in order to be like the image that is portrayed by these "stars"? What do we really know about who they are? Have we bowed or are we bowing to the satanic image without even realising it? If we refuse to bow to the image, then the only other option is to face the fire. Fire in scripture is used to represent persecution or suffering (see 1 Peter 4:12). If we refuse to bow to the image, we will face persecution in some shape or form. We have a decision to make–to bow or not to bow. I want to encourage you that you do not have to bow to the image, you do not have to fit in, and you do not have to surrender to the pressure to conform to the image of the world. We are exhorted not to conform to the world but to be transformed (Rom. 12:2). We are special, let us not be ashamed of who we are; let us embrace our peculiarity, because we are unique in the eyes of God. When we take a stand for God and refuse to bow to the image, He will reveal Himself in the fire.

Conclusion

I began writing this book when I was about eighteen years old, mainly following Minister Jeremy Grant's encouragement. I have experienced many things since I started writing this book, which is one of the reasons it took so long to finish it. I still have the same jovial personality, but life experiences have changed me from the naïve young man I was when I started writing. If the Lord tarries and my life is spared, I hope to be able to write more books to encourage the *Body of Christ*. I would like to leave you with a few words of advice and encouragement.

A. Find Out Who You Are in God

One of the reasons we struggle is because we do not know who we are in God. The only way we are going to find out is by getting to know God for ourselves through fasting and prayer.

B. Spend Time in the Word of God and Start Early

I have grown to where I am now because, from a young age, I developed a desire for the Word of God. The younger you are; the better and the sooner you begin, the more beneficial it will be for you long term (see 2 Tim. 3:15).

C. Knowledge Applied Is Greater than Knowledge Acquired

It is one thing to gain knowledge through studying or listening to the spoken Word, but it is another to apply what we have learned to our life. I encourage you to learn as much as you can. The Scriptures were written for our learning (Romans 15:4). If we consistently apply what we learn to our daily life, we will experience growth. Many Christians are still immature because they fail to apply what they have read or heard.

D. Never Forget Where You Are Coming From

We should never forget from where we are coming. I know I probably would not be teaching as I am today, if Evangelist Louisa Sinclair (nee Brade) had not given me the opportunity to teach the Youth Class in Sunday School when I was 18 years old. I did not realize that teaching would be a part of my ministry until she gave me the opportunity.

E. Stay Close to Your Spiritual Parents

Cling to your spiritual mothers and fathers in the Gospel. If you feel you do not have any, 'adopt one.' Seek them out and spend time with them. Listen to their testimonies that will challenge you to know God for yourself. One of my spiritual fathers in the Gospel is Elder Stone (I call him Elder Tarmac). Before I migrated to Canada, I would spend time with him. We have prayed, fasted, laughed, and cried together. As I grew up, whenever I was invited to minister at another church I would always ask him to accompany me as my covering.

I pray this book encourages you to embrace the sovereign call of God that is upon your life and always remember—You Are Not Normal.

Bibliography

Conner, K. J. (1992). *Interpreting the Symbols and Types.* Portland, OR: City Christian Publishing.

Hammond, F. (2011), *Soul-Ties.* Kirkwood, MO: Impact Christian Books

Kiyosaki, R. T. (2011). *Rich Dad, Poor Dad.* Scottsdale, AZ: Plata Publishing.

McCoy, R. A. (2011). Soul Ties: Breaking up with a Past That's Killing your Future. Brandon, MS: FaytheWorks Publishing, LLC

Tulloch, S. (1996), *Oxford Dictionary and Thesaurus.* Oxford, NY: Oxford University Press.

Tenny, T. F. (1998). *God Chasers "My Soul Follows Hard After Thee."* Shippensburg, PA: Destiny Image Publishers.

Unger, M. F. (1957). *The New Unger Bible Dictionary.* Chicago, IL: The

Moody Bible Institute of Chicago.

Webster, M. (2014). *Merriam-Webster's Collegiate Dictionary (11th ed.).* Versailes, KY: Library of Congress.

Word Aflame Press. (2014) *The Apostolic Study Bible,* Hazelwood, MO: Word Aflame Press.

Zodhiates, S. (1991). *The Hebrew-Greek Key Word Study Bible,* Chattanooga, TN: AMG International Inc.

About the Author

Shaun was born and raised in the UK as a member of Bethel United Church of Jesus Christ (Apostolic) UK. He served his local church in Birmingham as a teacher in the Sunday School Department and also the New Converts Class. He has also served the Youth Department on a local, district, and national level. He currently resides in Calgary, Alberta with his wife Sheryl. He prays that what you have read in this book has encouraged and challenged you and asks for your continued prayers that God will be glorified in his life.

End Notes

1. Traditional Central Asian style outer garment that covers the entire body and has a grille over the face that the woman looks through.
2. By entering a vineyard, Samson was challenging his Nazarite vow (see Judges 13:7, 14)
3. A spiritual/emotional connection you have to someone after being intimate with them, usually engaging in sexual intercourse. A soul tie can be formed without engaging in sexual intercourse.
4. A publican was a scribe who was appointed by local businessman to collect taxes on his behalf. The publicans would often charge more than the legal tax, keeping the rest for themselves and their employers. He would in turn give the money to the Roman government.
5. The press is another name for the crowd or multitude.
6. Lentil soup.
7. We know this because he worked a total of fourteen years for Laban's two daughters (Leah and Rachel) and a further six years for his cattle.
8. The man is identified by Jacob as God (Gen. 42:30) but Hosea identifies Him as the angel of God (Hos. 12:3–4).
9. Paul was a name the Gentiles would have been accustomed to

10. Stephen was one of the first deacons chosen by the disciples to help with the daily distribution of food (Acts 6:1–7).
11. Before they were called Christians, followers of Christ were known as "disciples," "saints," "the church," "believers," or followers of "the way."
12. The sin offering also allowed flour to be offered but only if the offerer was so poor that he couldn't afford two turtledoves or two pigeons (Lev. 5:11–13).
13. A tall four-sided stone column that becomes narrower towards the top and ends at a point.

CPSIA information can be obtained
at www.ICGtesting.com
Printed in the USA
LVOW01s0920030516
486379LV00007B/35/P